The Hidden Hand of American Hegemony

A volume in the series

Cornell Studies in Political Economy

EDITED BY PETER J. KATZENSTEIN

A full list of titles in the series appears at the end of the book.

The Hidden Hand
of American Hegemony

PETRODOLLAR RECYCLING AND
INTERNATIONAL MARKETS

DAVID E. SPIRO

CORNELL UNIVERSITY PRESS

Ithaca and London

First published 1999 by Cornell University Press

Library of Congress Cataloging-in-Publication Data

Spiro, David E.

The hidden hand of American hegemony : petrodollar recycling and international
markets / David E. Spiro
p.   cm. — (Cornell studies in political economy)
Includes index.
ISBN 0-8014-2884-X (cloth : alk. paper)
1. Balance of payments—Arab countries. 2. Investments, Arab. 3. Petroleum products—
Prices. 4. International finance. 5. Organization of Petroleum Exporting Countries.
6. International Monetary Fund. 7. United States—Foreign economic relations. I. Title.
II. Series.
HG3883.A67S64   1999
381'.17'0973—dc21   99-22900

Printed in the United States of America

Cloth printing 10 9 8 7 6 5 4 3 2 1

This book is dedicated to my teachers,
Robert G. Gilpin Jr. and Robert C. Tucker.

They provided me with intellectual capital,
and I am recycling the interest.

Contents

Preface

G. K. Chesterton once wrote, "It is the test of a good religion whether you can joke about it."[1] In 1974, U.S. Treasury Secretary William Simon was putting Islam through its paces. He flew on a government plane to Saudi Arabia to meet with the minister of finance because he was worried about the future of the international financial system and the place of the United States in it. Simon had put an extremely violent video on the in-flight movie system and he was laughing uproariously while consuming prodigious amounts of whiskey. Alcohol is illegal in Saudi Arabia, though drinking it might seem the national pastime to a new visitor in the Kingdom. Ministers of state are not supposed to roll off their planes drunk, but according to another government official on the trip, that is just what Simon did.

In 1974 the financial problems facing the U.S. secretary of the treasury were enough to drive any level-headed soul to his cups. The federal government was running an ever-increasing budget deficit, and it was Simon's job to finance it. By the end of the year the Treasury was "preempting 62 percent of the debt markets in this country," and Simon called the cost of paying interest on the national debt "just frightening."[2]

At the same time, the price of oil was getting higher and higher. Financial markets were in danger of collapse, partly because of new inflows of capital from oil-exporting nations. "The strains could be relieved," Simon thought, "if the . . . OPEC nations put a larger amount

---

[1] "Spiritualism," p. 149. I thank "The Quotemeister" at the American Chesterton Society (http://www.chesterton.org) for tracking down the source.

[2] U.S. Congress, Senate, Committee on Finance, *Economic Implications*, pp. 18, 19, and 24.

of their accumulated funds into investment in this country, or if the American public spends less and saves more."[3] Since it was unlikely that President Richard Nixon, while facing impeachment, would succeed in urging the public to spend less and save more, Simon turned to the Organization of Petroleum Exporting Countries (OPEC) for funding.

Before his appointment to public office, Simon had been a very successful bond salesman. (He also swam for the army in the Pacific Olympics during his tour of duty in Japan from 1946 to 1948.) At the age of twenty-five he joined Union Securities, where he traded municipal bonds. Five years later he was made a vice-president at Weeden and Company, and by 1970 (at the relatively tender age of forty-three) he was made a senior partner in charge of the Government Bond Department at Solomon Brothers.

Richard Nixon appointed Simon to the post of deputy secretary of the treasury in 1972, and after a short stint as "energy czar" during the height of the Arab oil embargo, Simon replaced George Shultz as treasury secretary in May 1974. Among the major achievements cited on the Simon Papers home page at Lafayette College (he would donate his papers to his alma mater) was his reintroduction of the two-dollar bill.[4]

His answer to the myriad problems faced by the Treasury—and by the United States in general, and indeed by most of the world—was to sell bonds. In 1974, Simon negotiated a secret deal so the Saudi central bank could buy U.S. Treasury securities outside of the normal auction. A few years later, Treasury Secretary Michael Blumenthal cut a secret deal with the Saudis so that OPEC would continue to price oil in dollars. These deals were secret because the United States had promised other industrialized democracies that it would not pursue such unilateral policies.

What was the challenge to U.S. interests, and to international financial and monetary stability, that so frightened these men? Was it the actions of the U.S. government, or the agreements made in international regimes, or the workings of international financial markets that answered this challenge?

John Kenneth Galbraith coined the term *Conventional Wisdom* to describe a view that is pervasive and widely believed—and absolutely wrong. The conventional wisdom on petrodollar recycling holds that in-

---

[3] U.S. Congress, Senate, Committee on Finance, *Effect of Petrodollars*, pp. 11–12.
[4] Http://www.lafayette.edu/library/special/simon/bio.html.

ternational capital markets acted as an intermediary between OPEC nations with capital surpluses and less developed countries (LDCs) that required balance-of-payments financing to fund higher oil import bills.
Insofar as this view imputes causation where there is none, ignores lines
of causation that are important, and generalizes improperly from a few
nations to an aggregate of many, it is decidedly incorrect.

A significant portion of the OPEC surplus was invested in U.S. government obligations. The funds that were placed in international capital markets did not change the growth trends of those markets. The expression commonly found in the literature, "banks were flush with
petrodollars," is unjustified. Only a small number of LDCs received the
bulk of new credit from banks. It is improper to generalize from this
very small number to say that LDCs in general received funding from international capital markets in the 1970s.

Balance-of-payments support for LDCs came from traditional (i.e., official) sources. The money that international bankers lent went to half a
dozen newly industrialized countries (NICs), the nations associated with
the debt crisis of the 1980s, and that debt paid for imports from the five
largest industrialized economies.

Industrialized nations defined *cooperation* in response to the oil crisis
as collusion to keep prices down. Authoritative mechanisms for the allocation of value (such as cooperating to suppress the "market" price of
oil) were the conventions that framed international power relationships. American policies violated cooperative agreements because they
were unilateral. The United States sought to justify its policies as "letting
markets work," even though markets had not previously been empowered as legitimate sources for balance-of-payments adjustment financing.

U.S. policy makers defined the legitimate response to the oil shock as
cooperating to accept a share of the trade deficit imposed by OPEC and
sharing the capital surplus of OPEC to finance those deficits. Yet U.S.
recruitment of Saudi funds was both the predominant mode of recycling and divergent from legitimate norms as perceived by U.S. policy
makers.

It is not the thesis of this book that policy makers in a hegemonic
state constantly intervene to pursue "rational" strategies. The empirical
evidence presented in Chapter 5 suggests that the United States followed the course of these policies without having a grand strategy. In
many instances, "letting the market work" meant that transnational actors were producing outcomes favorable to the United States.

This book asks how in practice petrodollars were recycled from oil-exporting states with a capital surplus to states with a trade deficit resulting from higher oil prices from 1973 to 1981. I examine three competing answers: market forces, international institutions, and hegemonic stability—as well as the null hypothesis of anarchy. A large amount of petrodollars did flow through capital markets, but not in a way that recycled funds from surplus states to economies with deficits. Instead, markets produced outcomes consistent with the international distribution of capabilities. International institutions such as the International Monetary Fund (IMF) attempted to play a role in recycling petrodollars, but were prevented by competition from the United States and by the failure of advanced industrialized democracies to abide by summitry agreements. American hegemony played the greatest role in recycling petrodollars; yet the nature of American policies violated the intersubjective agreements that defined the legitimate allocation of value in the international political economy.

This book began as an empirical investigation into petrodollar recycling and has ended as an attempt to reconcile realism and constructivism. Constructivism has been taken up by liberal and Marxist theorists, but few realists have paid it heed. (There are, of course, notable exceptions, such as Ted Hopf and Iain Johnston, and, although he may not identify himself as a constructivist-realist, Eric Helleiner.)[5] As a school of critical theory, constructivism is more an approach than an explanatory theory. Its liberal and Marxist adherents have used constructivism to reconfirm the basic tenets with which they started. I believe that realism is a similarly useful and powerful theory, one well served by adding constructivist approaches.

I wish to reconcile realism and constructivism because in some sense the two are antithetical. Constructivists believe that possible and observed worlds have equal truth value. By naming something, we endow it with reality. Realists, on the other hand, tend to believe that there is some objective reality waiting to be named. Naming, or speech, is for them a matter of observation and does not change empirical fact.

I take the middle ground, which may violate some of the ontological and epistemological foundations of constructivism but enriches and lends efficacy to realism. Rather than see an objective reality that is waiting to be named, I believe that world politics consists of socially con-

---

[5] Hopf, "Realism and Constructivism"; Johnston, *Cultural Realism*; and Helleiner, "National Currencies."

structed relationships. To study the core elements of realism, power and interests, we need to understand the intersubjective framework in which power and interests are embedded. It is possible to observe power and interests empirically, but it is difficult and misleading to interpret what we observe if the observations are taken out of their social context.

"Imagining international relations," I hold, has little utility and gives no help to analysts who wish to achieve the objectives of social science: explanation and post facto prediction. Constructivism has as its goal the reconstruction of international relations by recognizing new possibilities and empowering those imagined possibilities by considering them on equal ground with what is (or what has already been "named"). I have little sympathy and limited patience with this agenda. My goal, instead, is to recognize that "what is" has been created by a combination of purposive and accidental human agency. Power and interests, markets and authority, do not well from some natural law as does gravity. They are social constructs, and they must be studied as such.

In ignoring the subjectivity and intersubjectivity inherent in power and interests, markets and authority, realists have been lashed to a crag of rationalism. *The Hidden Hand of American Hegemony* is about the exercise of American power as structural change released policy makers from the constraints of legitimate authority. In that sense, the unbinding of hegemony from legitimacy finds little favor with most of our normative concerns. Yet the "unbinding of hegemony" has a second meaning, which is more congruent with Aeschylus' original title. In this book I hope to free realist theory from its shackles of rationalism and economic utilitarianism. Realism is an efficacious theory, particularly in its classical form, which paid attention to such concepts as legitimacy and norms. I do not subscribe to the importance of norms as causal influences. But neither do I think that power and interests can be recognized, interpreted, and understood except within their normative frameworks.

My ideas for this book have developed and (I hope) matured over the past fifteen years. My research on petrodollar recycling has not been static, but where I rely on interviews with policy makers I have tried to cite the earliest interview I conducted with each person. Usually, the policy maker's memory of petrodollar recycling was more clear in the 1980s than it was in the 1990s, and the stories they told were more nearly free of post hoc rationalizations. Very little of my general argument rests on personal interviews and unpublished documents, but where they contribute to the narrative I do not hestitate to use them. This tactic may at first seem awkward to the reader of an academic treatise, but I do not think it improper. It might be possible to cite journalistic sources in place of my own interviews, but to be immodest, I have greater trust in my own research than in the quick analysis of a journalist under deadline pressure. Except in a very few cases, the people I interviewed are cited by name, and other researchers can repeat the interviews to verify what I found. I have tried to identify unpublished documents as carefully as possible so that future researchers can request them under the Freedom of Information Act.

In researching and writing this book, I incurred more debt than some of the nations I describe. Time and funds and places to think and write and rewrite were provided by the Ford Foundation Program on West European Security, the Center for International Affairs at Harvard University, and National Endowment for the Humanities grants at Columbia University. Many people read and commented on parts of the manuscript, and I am extremely grateful to Hayward Alker, Robert Art, James Caporaso, Richard ("Ike") Eichenberg, Robert G. Gilpin, Robert Jervis, Ethan Kapstein, Peter Katzenstein, Friedrich Kratochwil, Edward D. Mansfield, Kenneth Oye, John Waterbury, Steven Weber, and John Wooding. I also owe great thanks to Cornell University Press editor Roger Haydon, who was an extraordinary nag during the four years after my contractual deadline for submitting this manuscript but helpful nonetheless. My greatest debt is to my spouse, Paulette Kurzer, who gave me time and support to research and write this book, at the same time that she taught full time, published her own book in this series, and parented two children. My children, Ezra and Katya, did not help at all, but I want to mention them anyway.

DAVID E. SPIRO

Tucson, Arizona

The Hidden Hand of American Hegemony

CHAPTER ONE

Explaining Petrodollar Recycling

The successful resolution of the disequilibrium in global balance of payments caused by the oil price revolution was one of the most remarkable achievements of the postwar era. Nearly 500 billion petrodollars were recycled from oil producers with a capital surplus to countries with trade deficits. A major threat to the international economic system was overcome, and the stability of that system was preserved. This book asks how the challenge of recycling petrodollars was successfully resolved.

The problem started in the early 1970s, when the Organization of Petroleum Exporting Countries raised the price of oil.[1] In 1970 the world price of crude oil was $1.80 per barrel. By 1980 it had reached $39.[2] OPEC nations could not possibly increase imports as fast as their export revenues rose (in 1978 alone they received $133.5 billion for oil exports), and no oil-consuming government wanted them to decrease oil exports. Thus OPEC ran a surplus on its trade of goods and services (the current account), and that surplus meant that the rest of the world ran a net deficit.

Recycling petrodollars was the process by which the oil exporters' surplus financed deficits elsewhere in the world. Recycling challenged cooperation among the advanced industrialized democracies and the stability of the international economic system in the distribution of trade deficits (which meant avoiding competitive trade policies) and in

[1] OPEC comprises Algeria, Ecuador, Gabon, Indonesia, Iran, Iraq, Kuwait, Libya, Nigeria, Qatar, Saudi Arabia, the United Arab Emirates (or UAE, formerly the Trucial States), and Venezuela.
[2] Blair, *Control of Oil*; and Yergin, *Prize*, p. 784.

the distribution of capital (i.e., avoiding competition for OPEC investments).

Henry Kissinger saw the problem as similar to that which caused the Great Depression because governments would be tempted to implement policies such as "exchange rate depreciation, import restriction, export subsidization, controls on capital outflow, and interest rate or other incentives to encourage capital inflow." Yet if each nation pursued similar policies, none would work, and the policies would lead to a competitive wave of restrictive measures or bidding for capital that would risk a serious drop in world trade, a deflationary downspiral, and possibly worldwide depression.[3] Similarly, William Casey predicted that this crisis could "threaten the world with a vicious cycle of competition, autarky, rivalry, and depression such as led to the collapse of the world order in the thirties."[4]

Central bankers in the United States worried that international financial markets might collapse. In a secret meeting with officials of the Treasury Department in the summer of 1974, a New York Federal Reserve official expressed alarm that the market between banks had "dried up," and smaller banks were shut out of the interbank market. He said that "all the ingredients for financial chaos were there," and "the New York Fed was placing bank rescue at the top of its priorities, as was the Bank of England."[5] Publicly, the chairman of the Federal Reserve Board of Governors noted that petrodollar recycling "is fraught with danger for the stability of international financial markets. It is by no means clear that private markets will be able to recycle the huge surpluses."[6]

Oil exporters had a structural trade surplus because they could not increase their imports as fast as the price of oil rose. Thus there had to be a trade deficit elsewhere in the world.[7] If one oil-importing nation attempted to boost its exports so that its trade account would come into

---

[3] Casey, "International Economic Affairs in 1974 [a speech made before the Public Affairs Council at Washington on February 28 (press release 75)]," reprinted in Department of State, *Bulletin* 70, no. 1813, 25 March 1974; p. 304.

[4] Department of State, *Bulletin* 70, no. 1810, 4 March 1974; p. 201.

[5] Keyser to Willett.

[6] Statement by Arthur Burns before the Joint Economic Committee of the U.S. Congress. Federal Reserve *Bulletin*, July 1974, p. 563.

[7] If there are only two countries in the world, and one has a trade surplus with the second, then Country 1 is selling more goods and services than it buys while Country 2 is buying more than it sells. If we divide the world into OPEC and the rest of the world, then if OPEC has a trade surplus, there must be a corresponding trade deficit in the rest of the world.

balance, it would simply shift the deficit to another nation. If every nation had attempted to do so, none would have succeeded because there had to be a deficit. The result would have been a damaged regime for international trade with a net loss in welfare for all.

Oil-importing countries had to have oil for their economies to function. Since they could not buy less oil, and since OPEC could not import as many goods and services as the new price of oil now bought, OPEC had to have a trade surplus. The question was, Who would get stuck with the corresponding deficit? Each individual nation had an incentive to bring its trade account into balance, but all would have been better off if they cooperated to accept the structural trade deficit.

The challenge of how capital would be distributed was almost a mirror image of the challenge of preventing trade wars. Once nations agreed to share the trade deficit, there was a danger that they would compete for petrodollars to fund those deficits.[8] Even if there was untroubled cooperation among oil importers, an additional problem entailed reaching an agreement with oil exporters on where to place their assets. This challenge to the international monetary system was described by the director of research for the General Agreement on Tariffs and Trade (GATT), Jan Tumlir. He modeled a world with an oil exporter A, and three oil importers U, J, and E. Exporter A raises the price of oil and keeps the additional proceeds in monetary assets, which are E's Euro, J's Jen, and "U's currency (which, just to break the monotony, may be called the dollar)."[9] If A decides to hold dollars indefinitely, U would be able to print money to pay for oil and to lend to E and J with no real consequence. Exporter A would be trading oil for pieces of paper, and E and J would borrow that paper at little cost.

It is not certain, however, that A will indefinitely hold dollars rather than using them to claim goods and services from the oil-importing economies. As Tumlir noted, A is giving a double loan to U, for the time being. U is not forced to produce more or to reduce consumption for the more expensive oil, and it receives E and J's increased oil costs in the form of goods and services. Yet this arrangement is only for the time being, and it requires the active cooperation of all parties involved. E and J must not vie for capital inflows from A, and U must accept a current account deficit (as well as the effects of foreign capital in its money

---

[8] Again, by definition, a deficit in the current account is offset by a deficit in the capital account. Money must flow out of a country in order to pay for the goods and services it buys, and in order to earn that money a nation must sell securities or debt.

[9] Tumlir, "Oil Payments," p. 41.

markets). If U tries to defend its current account, Tumlir predicted, it "would lead to a cumulative downward spiraling of trade and income among the three."[10] In sum, the challenge was to convince oil exporters to hold capital surpluses in monetary form, while effecting cooperation among the oil importers.

Clearly, this arrangement would have been advantageous for the United States. It could print dollars in exchange for both oil and the goods of Europe and Japan. So why did not every nation try to do the same? The answer is that not every nation had the capacity to print its currency in exchange for oil and for foreign trade. But even if other nations did have that capacity, if every state had competed for the privilege of printing money to pay for oil, all would have had to convince OPEC to hold their currencies or to accept deficits from other oil importers. This strict matching of trade and capital flows would not have been likely or feasible.

For the sake of the stability of the international monetary system, only one nation could have assumed the role of providing a key currency for recycling. Without such leadership, there was a strong possibility of mutually destructive competition for capital. Yet this form of leadership also carried with it the potential for exorbitant privileges. If the United States competed for capital unilaterally, and then made other nations come to terms for access to that capital, the result would be predatory leadership that was not in anyone's interest except that of the United States.

Access to capital enabled nations to adjust gradually. If consumer nations had simply bought less oil and tightened their belts, then OPEC would not have had a surplus. But sudden adjustment would have displaced large sectors of the economy and would have caused an economic downturn more severe than anything we have witnessed in the postwar era. Gradual adjustment meant that consumer nations had time to adopt energy conservation measures and slowly get used to tightening their belts. Rather than put a big proportion of the population out of work, politicians were able to hide the adjustment in lower real wages and higher inflation.

Mechanisms that allow gradual adjustment to large economic shocks are crucially important. Balance-of-payments adjustment mechanisms are the elements regimes use to allow national leaders to abide by the rules of an international monetary system. Without balance-of-payments

[10] Ibid., p. 43.

adjustment financing, the resort to protectionist or nationalistic policies that violate the international monetary order is too attractive for politicians to avoid.

Under the Bretton Woods system, nations were given an incentive to stay with pegged rates (or at least less of a disincentive) through the International Monetary Fund, an organization based on the organizing principles of wealth, power, and, in small part, liberal democracy. To the extent that the IMF differed from a reification of the power hierarchy of its constituent parts, it was that the advanced industrialized democracies held a disproportionately large vote, and the number of votes required to annul decisions kept shrinking as the U.S. voting share shrank.

Little was left to markets when balance-of-payments adjustment financing was carried out by the IMF. The Eurodollar market did not exist until 1958, and its exponential growth became noticeable only in the 1970s. No other mechanisms existed for balance-of-payments adjustment financing except for official development assistance (foreign aid) and loans from the domestic branches of commercial banks. Both were ad hoc in character, and they could not be relied on when the economy turned sour—which was precisely the time that balance-of-payments adjustment financing is most needed.[11]

Recycling, then, is a case study of balance-of-payments adjustment financing for the period just after the collapse of the Bretton Woods agreement. It represents the nature of the changing international monetary system and how nations financed balance of payments adjustment following the closing of the gold window. How the international political economy distributes balance-of-payments adjustment financing is particularly important as the globe moves toward more tightly integrated banking markets. And it is of special concern to citizens of the United States, who have come to depend on foreign capital to keep the economy moving.

In the case of petrodollar recycling and the challenges it presented in the arenas of international trade and capital flows, market outcomes would have been less than desirable. Where the price mechanism consists of the supplies and demands of national governments, markets would have led to a decrease in general welfare. Cooperation among the advanced industrial democracies was a polite word for collusion to

---

[11] Cohen, *Organizing the World's Money*. On the role of countercyclical lending in international economic stability, see Kindleberger, "Dominance and Leadership."

fix prices. Oil, trade with OPEC, and the distribution of OPEC investments was to be set by political agreement. Inherent in all of the challenges presented by petrodollar recycling is the tension between market
mechanisms and political authority in allocating value.

CONTENDING EXPLANATIONS OF PETRODOLLAR RECYCLING

Market Forces

Neoclassical economists believe that the price mechanism, which allocates goods by the most efficient means possible, comes about automatically when individuals are permitted free access to supply and demand. Markets are seen as a primitive (though highly desirable) state,
which comes about naturally and thrives in the absence of interference
by politicians. Our mode of exchange is by markets whether we know it
or not, according to Paul Samuelson. Samuelson compares our understanding of markets to the way Jourdain felt about prose in *Le bourgeois
gentihomme:* "By my faith! for over forty years I've been speaking prose
without knowing anything about it."[12] Whatever occurs in the absence of
authoritative allocation schemes is attributable to the immutable laws of
supply and demand.

When free markets are allowed to develop, international cooperation
and harmony are automatic. As each individual actor pursues his own
interest, all are better off. The absence of markets is signified either by
political authority or market failure. Because liberalism holds that the
individual is the seat of moral value, the world is better off when individuals are free to choose for themselves (i.e., without government intervention).[13] In the case of petrodollar recycling, government intervention might include protectionism, exchange and capital controls, and
the allocation of balance-of-payments adjustment financing by a mechanism based on something other than supply and demand. (The IMF
and the financial Safety Net devised by the OECD described in Chapter
4, and the secret agreements that are outlined in Chapter 5 are examples of this counterfactual to market forces.)

Market failure starts with a strong presumption that the price mechanism is and should be automatic. It describes situations in which goods
fail to clear markets or prices fail to differentiate between goods be-

---

[12] Samuelson, *Readings,* p. 20. The quote is from Molière, *Bourgeois gentihomme.*
[13] Hall, *Liberalism,* p. 2.

cause of imperfect information.[14] In order to say that markets fail, we must know what they "should" do, and this expectation is often more normative than objective. Market failure either contradicts our expectations of automaticity or else disabuses us of some notion of value. It is very difficult to specify precisely what the world would look like in the absence of market forces, but describing such a world is vital to any meaningful test of outcomes for market mechanisms.

Because the price mechanism is so intrinsic to what economists mean by market forces, it is often the case that whenever something takes place in the setting of an economic institution, the outcome is called "market forces at work." Economists were led to attribute market forces to the case of petrodollar recycling because much of the capital surpluses were deposited in banks. It was simply assumed that whatever happened was caused by the price mechanism because of the private nature of the depository institutions. Money placed in public institutions, such as aid agencies, was assumed to be allocated according to political authority.

There are two problems with this sort of prediction. First, the public/private nature of an institution does not necessarily tell us whether the outcome was owing to market forces or to political authority. Aid agencies often make loans that are only marginally different from those made in private capital markets (both in price and in structure), and banks often make loans for purely political reasons.[15] Second, this view boils down to the idea that whatever economic actors do is market forces. Falsification is hardly possible.

Institutions

Liberal institutionalism, as represented by scholars such as Robert Keohane, Douglass North, and Beth and Robert Yarbrough, accepts anarchy as a problematic and proposes that it is partially mitigated by international regimes and institutions.[16] The problem that liberal institu-

---

[14] Caporaso and Levine, *Theories of Political Economy.*

[15] The definition of *official development assistance* (ODA) includes loans that are made at interest rates that are only marginally lower than market rates. Thus, for example, a nation that borrowed money on concessional terms when market interest rates were high might end up paying $100 million in interest on a $200 million "concessional" loan. See, for example, Husayn, *Al-iqtisād,* 1: 164.

For examples of banks making loans for political motives, see Spindler, *Politics of International Credit.*

[16] Keohane, *International Institutions;* North, *Structure and Change;* and Yarbrough and

tionalism addresses is the difficulty nation-states have in reaching cooperative agreements, even when they share interests in cooperation. These problems are caused by the cost of information, transaction costs, and what is analogous to market failure. Institutions function to efface the problems caused by market failure. Were there no political institutions in the world, we would be beset by market failures and inefficiencies.

Though actors are assumed to intend rational action in liberal institutionalism, their rationality is bounded by both the high costs of processing voluminous flows of information and the difficulty of knowing what the future will bring. It is this bounded rationality and uncertainty that give institutions their function. Institutions lower transaction costs, make more transparent participant nations' compliance (or noncompliance), and serve as a focal point about which expectations can converge. In short, institutions give states an additional incentive to cooperate, and at the very least they make it easier to play by the rules of the system.

An underlying assumption of liberal institutionalism seems to be that because all states will be better off if each cooperates, there is a general "demand" for mechanisms that make cooperation easier. Further, if there is a demand, institutions that facilitate cooperation will be "supplied." Like the price mechanism, there exists some equilibrium between supply and demand where institutions will exist and will affect outcomes. Liberal institutionalist authors such as the Yarbroughs seem surprised that in the international political economy, "even potentially mutually beneficial relationships may require relatively complex institutional structures to support cooperation."[17] As with the large literature on the iterated Prisoners' Dilemma, the epistemology of liberal institutionalism begins by defining the problem as one of explaining cooperation and concludes by arguing that cooperation is automatic after all.[18]

An advantage of liberal institutionalism is that making predictions about petrodollar recycling is fairly straightforward. The theory would expect capital to be allocated through regimes. To the extent that institutions such as the IMF or the International Energy Agency (IEA) successfully recycled petrodollars, liberal institutionalism is confirmed. Further, to the extent that new institutions were necessitated by the

Yarbrough, "Free Trade." Joseph Nye suggested the term "liberal institutionalism" for Grieco, "Anarchy and the Limits of Cooperation."

[17] Yarbrough and Yarbrough, "International Institutions," p. 239.

[18] See Spiro, "State of Cooperation."

challenge of petrodollar recycling, the theory predicts that these new recycling mechanisms would lower transaction costs, provide information and transparency, and serve as loci for actors' expectations.

Hegemony

According to structural realists, stability in the international political economy is provided when one nation serves as a leader or "hegemon." Until World War I Great Britain served as the hegemon, and the United States has filled the role in the postwar period. Charles Kindleberger suggested that the hegemon fulfills three important functions as an international "stabilizer": maintaining an open market for distress goods, providing countercyclical long-term lending (and serving as a lender of last resort), and providing liquidity to the system.[19] In this view, the hegemon provided public goods: services to the international system that would otherwise be underprovided. As with other public goods in the international arena, the problem was that public goods invite free riding, and eventually their cost to the hegemon outweighs their benefit.

A more predatory version of hegemony is suggested in the works of Robert Gilpin, Stephen Krasner, and David Calleo.[20] For Gilpin, the hegemon consistently acts in its own interest, and it is only happy circumstance that places hegemonic policy in confluence with milieu goals for the international system.[21] Gilpin is profoundly pessimistic, and a portion of his theory is based on the notion that power corrupts. As the hegemonic nation gains power it becomes soft and spoiled, and the populace is increasingly hesitant to pay for the costs of maintaining the international system. Combined with a diffusion of power, wealth, and know-how from center to periphery, which results in a relative decline in hegemonic capabilities, the unwillingness to pay the cost of empire means that the hegemon becomes more exploitative of its position. This malevolent hegemony followed by a return to isolationism, the leitmotif of Calleo's policy proposals, leads to instability and autarky in the international political economy. The epistemology of realism is a willingness to be disappointed by world events. The schema for

---

[19] Kindleberger, *World in Depression*, p. 292.

[20] Gilpin, *War and Change*; Krasner, "State Power"; and Calleo, *Beyond American Hegemony*.

[21] Arnold Wolfers first wrote of the distinction between milieu goals and possession goals in foreign policy in *Discord and Collaboration; Essays on International Politics* (Baltimore: Johns Hopkins University Press, 1962), pp. 73–80.

world order, such as hegemony and domination, are not always the preferable result.[22]

Given the decline of the United States relative to other advanced industrialized economies during the 1970s, the structural realist explanation of petrodollar recycling predicts the distribution of petrodollars by a cooperative agreement that reflects the increasingly exploitative nature of American hegemony. A purely cooperative agreement would have meant that nations accepted a share of the structural deficit with OPEC, rather than competing to adjust their current accounts. The OPEC surplus would have been distributed among oil-importing nations so as to permit deficits. Petrodollars would have been recycled by authoritative mechanisms, such as the IMF and the OECD Safety Net, and the principles by which these mechanisms distributed petrodollars would have reflected the distribution of capabilities among the member nations.

Counterfactuals and Anarchy

Realism views anarchy as both a counterfactual for order and a fundamental characteristic of international relations. Nations exist in a "self-help" world, with no governing institutions, no monopoly on the legitimate use of force, and no means for enforcing rules and agreements.[23] In contradistinction to the ideal type of governance in civil society, international relations are characterized by the absence of institutions that are larger than the sum of their parts. Each state is on its own, and the distribution of capabilities determines who gets what, when, and where. It is this absence of governance that leads to the conflictual nature of international relations. Robert Gilpin observes: "As Thomas Hobbes told his patron, the 2nd Earl of Devonshire, and realist writers have always attempted to tell those who would listen, 'it's a jungle out there.' Anarchy is the rule; order, justice, and morality are the exceptions."[24]

The conflictual nature of international relations, stemming from the absence of a central government, leads realists to a second understanding of anarchy, which is more Hobbesian. In this version, anarchy means a lack of order and a chaotic state of continual war. This second understanding serves as a counterfactual for realists because the import

[22] Loriaux, "Realists and Saint Augustine."
[23] Bull, *Anarchical Society.*
[24] Gilpin, "Richness of the Tradition of Political Realism," p. 304.

of their theory is to explain order and the existence of stability. Given an expectation that chaos should ensue from a lack of governance, the question that motivates realism is why we observe peace, stability, and cooperation in international relations. If anarchy is the rule, and order is the exception, then realism is an explanation of exceptions.[25]

Neoclassical economics does not view anarchy as problematic because markets, and therefore the efficient allocation of resources, occur naturally. Liberal institutionalism is motivated by the problems of anarchy, which result from market failure, but the inefficient allocation of value is avoided once institutions ameliorate the absence of central governance.[26]

These three explanations are contending in the sense that the infirming of one suggests the confirming of another. If markets worked, then realism is infirmed and an institutional explanation is unnecessary. If petrodollars were distributed authoritatively and if market failure is the problematic that is solved by institutions, then both market-based explanations and realism are infirmed. Neoclassical economic theory and liberal institutionalism would be infirmed if the distribution of capital flows depended on the international distribution of power.

In addition to pitting these theories against one another, it is important to conduct a "veridical" test, which is to say we should test whether recycling did, in fact, take place.[27] Differing understandings of anarchy, and the possible infirming of theories by the confirming of another, make a veridical test difficult. The null hypothesis for each explanation is unique. It is therefore possible that by putting the three explanations in contention, we are making it impossible to observe a null hypothesis, which, in turn, makes it more likely that we will impute meaning to a series of events when it is possible that no meaning exists.

A true null hypothesis for all of the three contending theories would be a set of random outcomes that are not predicted or explainable by any of the theories. As a veridical test, this nonexplanation predicts that petrodollars were not recycled at all. Capital flows did not reflect the logic of market forces, or the authoritative allocative principles of institutions, or the international distribution of capabili-

---

[25] Waltz, *Theory of International Politics*; and Art and Jervis, "Anarchic Environment."

[26] Keohane, *International Institutions*.

[27] The term *veridical* is suggested by Willard V. Quine as a counterpart to falsidical paradoxes. In his usage, a veridical paradox is explained by a false sense of paradox, not by a false logical argument. As used here, a veridical test examines whether the question, and not the proposed explanation, is incorrect. See Quine, *Ways of Paradox*, pp. 3–20.

ties. This description fits a world in which recycling was not an element of balance-of-payments adjustment. We know that something happened after the oil shocks of the 1970s, but whether what happened merits systematic interpretation and explanation should be left open to question.

CONSTRUCTING A REALIST INTERPRETATION OF POWER

For petrodollar recycling, the cooperative scenario that structural realism predicts differs from liberal institutionalist outcomes because the public good of adjustment and stability is provided by American leadership. In the absence of such leadership, nations would compete for capital and to adjust their current accounts, with the result that all would be worse off. This prediction, however, comes from a static reading of hegemonic stability theory and does not take into account the declining relative position of the United States. The theory is confirmed in the fullest sense only if cooperative arrangements for petrodollar recycling represented a shift in U.S. policies from the milieu goals of international economic stability to the particularistic interests of the dominant yet declining hegemon. It is this shift in the nature of policies that we are unable to interpret using realist theory in its current form.

Even if the interpretation of evidence is agreed upon, neither hegemonic stability theory nor liberal institutionalism has been very good at specifying predicted outcomes. In part, this lack of specification of outcomes is responsible for the confusion over what should be the fairly incontrovertible fact of American decline. According to "antideclinist" theorists such as Samuel Huntington, Henry Nau, and Joseph Nye, even the basic observation that U.S. power is in decline relative to the rest of the world is subject to debate because we continue to see the successful use of American power.[28] When decline is measured by outcomes, rather than serving as an independent variable that predicts outcomes, the underlying indicators of decline are confused with the predicted results to which decline leads.

For Gilpin, decline should mean increasing closure in the world economy and increasing instability. Though increasing integration of national economies through interdependence would seem to contra-

[28] Huntington, "U.S.—Decline?"; Nau, *Myth of America's Decline*; Nye, *Bound to Lead*. An excellent evaluation of the debate over American decline is in Rosecrance, *America's Economic Resurgence*, chap. 2.

dict his predictions, he treats the globalization of world markets as exogenous to the model. Keohane shies away from any predictions, which makes the model nearly impossible to use as a research tool. The decline of U.S. power may be obviated by the possibility of functional regimes and institutions, which might produce cooperative outcomes.[29]

Referring to the Melian Dialogue, an old-time favorite of academic realists, Friedrich Kratochwil observes that during the recent changes in East Europe, "the strong suddenly realized that what they 'can' do was as different from the repertoire of politics as usual, and the weak noticed that the modality of 'must' was equally undergoing a nearly unheard of transformation." The changes, he points out, came from a new understanding of empowerment by mass movements that was simultaneous with a realization of powerlessness by leaders, yet "realism as a 'theory', stressing power as the crucial variable, had no way of comprehending this crisis"[30] These problems should serve as a heuristic to prompt new methods for interpretation. Our answer lies in reconstructing an interpretive framework that is rhetorically persuasive to the logical rigor of positivism, while embedding the analysis of power in its background of norms, values, social conventions, and social purpose.

Ideas about norms, legitimacy, and social conventions are often associated with liberal theorists, but realist theory has a long tradition of concern with such concepts.[31] If the primary focus of realism is power, and the theory's greatest shortcoming is an unsophisticated practice of power analysis, then it is squarely within the realist tradition to improve the theory by incorporating new ideas about power. Our understanding of power analysis is greatly improved by the work of David Baldwin, who explains that power is contingent on context and must be examined in specific frameworks.[32] For power to be a useful concept in theories of international relations, it cannot be generalized beyond specific contexts. Generalization, however, is what makes theories possible. If we can analyze power only on a case-by-case basis, our theories will be ad hoc by definition.

In Robert Dahl's well-known description, Leyla has power over Majnun to the extent that she can get him to do something he would not

[29] Kindleberger, "Hierarchy."

[30] Kratochwil, "World as a Shop," p. 2. See also Kratochwil, "Embarassment of Changes"; and Koslowski and Kratochwil, "Understanding Change."

[31] Carr, *Twenty Years' Crisis*; and Ikenberry and Kupchan, "Socialization."

[32] Baldwin, *Paradoxes*.

otherwise do.[33] Critics of Dahl argue that this description ignores un-intended consequences, which some theorists call "structural power."[34] They argue that the United States often acts in ways that affect other nations, even if the United States was not trying to get anyone to do anything. In 1979, for example, the Federal Reserve Board allowed domestic interest rates to rise, which had the unanticipated effect of contributing to the Third World debt crisis. They argue that such causal influences should not be excluded from our definition of power.[35]

Power as a concept is made more useful by restricting its definition to one category of causes. If power is synonymous with cause and effect, then power analysis embodies all forms of explanation. To preserve the distinction between power and explanation, we should also differentiate between power relationships and structural causes. One way of doing this is to require that Leyla intend to change Majnun's behavior. If a person abhors the color purple and therefore walks around a piece of purple plastic lying on the ground, it is a senseless dilution of the utility of power analysis to claim that the purple plastic has power. Plastic cannot have power over people. Similarly, if a purple person lying on the ground unknowingly repels the purplephobe, there is little reason to state that one has power over the other. If, however, the purple person discovers the effect he is having, and wishes to repel the person walking, then the relationship can be described as one of power. The point here is not to differentiate powerful people from purple plastic but rather to operationalize the concept of power as distinct from other forms of causation.

The behavioral definition of power is largely intersubjective, and what differentiates power from other forms of explanation is the presence of shared meanings. If the intent of Leyla (the powerholder) is important in describing power, the alternatives open to Majnun (the one affected by power) are the meat of power analysis. We must argue a reasonable counterfactual future that Majnun would have preferred to follow if we are to describe that outcome he finally did follow as the result of a power relationship. To describe something that Majnun would not have

[33] Dahl, "Concept of Power." He uses the terms "A" and "B," which are replaced here with names from classical Arabic love poetry to make life less tedious.

[34] Strange, "What about International Relations?"; and Caporaso and Haggard, "Power in International Political Economy."

[35] Indeed, some theorists have argued that the exclusion of this type of causation from definitions of power is a way to absolve the industrialized world from responsibility for un-intended acts. Power is understood to carry liability, whereas unintentional consequences may not.

otherwise done, we have to say what Majnun would have done in the absence of a power relationship.

The problem with placing the brunt of power analysis on this counterfactual future is that it burdens power analysis, which until now was a fairly nonideological method, with normative baggage. The counterfactual future for Majnun is a sort of null hypothesis for power analysis, which implies that individuals have the ability to make choices and determine self-interest in the absence of power relationships. The idea that individuals are naturally endowed with freedom of action and choice and a set of utilities that are given deus ex machina is decidedly liberal. And put in these terms, it precludes as a subset of power relationships the influencing of autonomous desires and the socialization of norms and values.

The assertion that we can recognize and understand power outcomes as distinct from counterfactual futures is tantamount to an assertion that there could possibly be a counterfactual future uninfluenced by others (i.e., not a power relationship). If power relationships were normal in society; if our actions were in fact explainable as outcomes of power others hold over us; if power is a useful concept for understanding agency; then how would we know about a counterfactual future not subject to power? Why would our subjective consciousness even understand that such an alternative exists?

Leyla must understand that there is a difference between the outcome of power and the alternative future, or she would not be capable of intending to change Majnun's behavior. But if Leyla does not tell us about the alternative future (and it would not likely be in her strategic interest to do so), then the hidden logical presumption of Dahl's description is that analysts of power are (like Leyla) the holders of power—that is, we are politically privileged and empowered—or that there exist profound silences about power in society. The analyst of power, by describing a social interaction as a power relationship, reveals the counterfactual futures that might not have been apparent as reasonable alternatives.

A final element of analyzing power is establishing the causal link between Leyla's intent and Majnun's change in behavior. There has to be a causal link between the two, or else there is nothing to differentiate power from coincidence. The cause of a power outcome is an entirely subjective change. Consider as an example what happens when a mugger gives you a choice between giving him money or suffering harm. Many people would give money to a mugger once convinced that they face harm, but few would hand over their money in the absence of changed expectations. The coercive element of power in this case is a purely subjective change from a feeling of safety to a choice between safety and harm. As a victim, your counterfactual future is the expectation that you would be happiest keeping your money (or freely choosing to distribute it charitably). Once a subjective expectation of violence accompanies the counterfactual future, you will probably expect to be happiest giving up your money and thereby avoiding harm.

Having recognized that the study of power necessarily entails the study of subjectivity and intersubjectivity, it makes sense that we cannot recognize power outcomes or understand their meaning until we place them in the context of shared norms. In the case of the mugging, the set of expectations that originally led the victim to feel safe in the absence of a threat by the mugger derived entirely from a set of social conventions about law, property rights, and the appropriate circumstances for money to change hands. It is the violation of these social conventions that frame mugging as a power outcome.

The mutual agreement that economic exchange is appropriate for the distribution of goods depends on social convention. There are many instances (buying votes, for instance) in which economic exchange is not deemed to be legitimate. If a teacher insists that A grades in a course will go to the highest bidder, the outcome represents both market forces and power. The only way that we as observers can meaningfully differentiate between the two is when we take into account the normative framework that makes meritocracy and hard work legitimate bases for distributing academic grades. Whether market outcomes are the result of a legitimate system for allocation, an example of an actor intervening in a legitimate system of allocation so that markets produce the outcome (when politics should), or an example of a state intervening in the market itself (legitimately or not) depends on our ability to recognize shared intersubjective understandings.

To recognize market forces as a power outcome, and to differentiate between the predatory and benign exercise of power, we must put the outcome into an intersubjective context. The problem is how to observe intersubjective contexts objectively. This book is motivated in part by the fact that scholars have given widely divergent interpretations to the same set of outcomes. I seek to solve this quandary by setting the exercise of power within a normative framework of social purpose. But this solution will have little utility if we cannot objectively observe a normative framework of social purpose.

John Ruggie has written: "The way to test theories of international cooperation is to pick an important case that is representative of other cases, and test the case for deviations from acceptability in the 'context of intersubjective . . . meaning.' "[36]

Studying perceptions and intersubjectivity is not as convincing as "hard facts" to an audience steeped in the pseudo-positive tradition. Yet structures, Anthony Giddens has observed, exist only insofar as human agents react to them.[37] By the same token, the problem of recycling petrodollars and the problem of policy coordination were problematic only insofar as they were defined as such or constrained the actions of policy makers.

If intersubjectivity is to be a baseline for measuring how systemic constraints affect agency, however, the question remains as to how one can discern and describe state actions from within the intersubjective consciousness of policy makers' conceptions of an international system. A fairly elegant and parsimonious approach to this problem has been suggested by Robert C. Tucker. He calls for breaking into the complex myriad of the polity by examining the way political leaders perceive and define problems calling for political action.[38] With leadership as a focal point, we need not necessarily posit the importance of leadership as politics (as does Tucker), but by the same token such a method does not arbitrarily impute importance or causality to any single element of the political process. Leadership is simply a way of breaking into the political cycle.

In Tucker's paradigm, political leadership consists of three stages. First, the leader defines a situation. Given the continuum of nondiscrete events over time in the polity, there is often no objective measure for what constitutes a situation requiring political response or the time frame of the situation. It is the leader's definition of the situation that later determines policies and their effectiveness. In the second stage of Tucker's paradigm the leader formulates a policy response to the situation, and mobilizes support for it. In the third stage leaders implement the policy. The trick for the academic researcher is to differentiate between statements that are made to define situations and those that are made to mobilize support for a policy's implementation. Statements need to be differentiated according to source and content.

Understanding conceptions of legitimate action is much more difficult because the political actor may not be fully aware of how she understands social purpose. One way to approach this problem is to ana-

---

[36] Ruggie, "International Regimes." For this passage, Ruggie cites Chomsky, *Current Issues in Linguistic Theory* (Hague: Mouton, 1964), chap. 1.

[37] Giddens, *Central Problems.*

[38] Tucker, *Politics as Leadership.*

lyze the statements of public officials as they attempt to explain and justify their policies. In cases of perceived conflict, public statements avow-
ing cooperative intent are useful to the researcher because they reveal
the norms and principles of accepted behavior to which the policy
maker is appealing. These norms are, in essence, a form of shared language for agreement on what constitutes legitimate domination.
Through such rhetoric, the policy maker seeks to cloak an illegitimate
action in the shared language of accepted norms. Thus the public statement that contradicts true intent can serve to identify those norms. Furthermore, delineating such a contradiction helps us to measure the extent of congruity between authority relationships in international
relations.[39] The more incongruous shared language and policy formula-
tion by the leading power are, the greater is the likelihood of instability
in international relations in the future.

This method of analysis rests on the claim that there exists a set of objective indicators signaling policy makers' perceptions and intents.
None of these genres of sources—public statements, research interviews, and classified memoranda—is perfectly objective indicators of
policy makers' perceptions, but treating them as evidence is better than
etiolating evidential proof. To a large degree, the thesis that a situation
was perceived as conflictual and competitive, or that a policy was meant
to be noncooperative and exploitative, must rest on the skill of the author's argumentation and familiarity with the subject matter. The study
of empirical evidence in international relations is never a truly objective
science, but it is most compelling when clearly, carefully, and logically
argued.

[39] This methodology is from Eckstein, *Division and Cohesion*, esp. Appendix B.

CHAPTER TWO

Defining the Principles of Allocation

This chapter explores the problem American policy makers perceived in petrodollar recycling, the threats of that problem to international cooperation, and the meaning of that threat to the shared concept of international legitimacy. I examine the agreed-upon and legitimate roles of authoritative leadership and of international markets in distributing balance-of-payments financing (and petrodollars in particular). What was considered legitimate, and what constituted illegitimate intervention in the system?

My purpose is twofold. First, by exposing the intersubjective understandings by which policy makers understood legitimacy, I establish a baseline by which to compare their actions. It is not possible to claim that actions are illegitimate without first establishing what would be legitimate. Second, it is not possible to interpret power outcomes in a vacuum: one must observe the intersubjective framework in which policies take place in order to identify when power takes place.

Though recycling was defined as a problem by policy makers throughout the world, I consider only the reactions of officials in the United States in an effort to examine the ontology of cooperation and illegitimacy. To argue that the United States provided a public good of recycling and exploited its dominant economic position in the international system in doing so, I must demonstrate that recycling was perceived to be a public good, establish the place of recycling in the context of hegemonic legitimacy, and evidence the divergence of U.S. actions from that baseline of legitimacy. Because U.S. actions play the crucial role in this argument, it is U.S. perceptions with which I am concerned. I follow the method of analyzing the statements of public officials that I outlined in

Chapter 1. Using Robert C. Tucker's focus on how leaders define situations, we begin to understand how policy makers framed the set of available policy responses to the situation. To interpret those policies, I set them in the framework of shared norms and social conventions of legitimacy. The problem is to observe objectively intersubjective constructions, which I do by examining the justificatory statements that policy makers made in public. Public statements by officials rarely tell us anything about the true motivation for their actions. But public statements—especially those before congressional committees—are often offered as justifications for policies. When officials offer justification, they must refer to shared understandings of legitimacy, or else the justification fails. Thus we can study public statements for what they tell us about legitimacy, even if the underlying policies are illegitimate.

This method is similar to the "forensic attestation" method used by Edward E. Cohen in his fascinating study of Athenian banking. Because the historical data on how Athenians made loans and charged interest are sketchy and controversial, Cohen examined the records of ancient court cases involving lending. He did not examine the actual lending practices that were subject to litigation but instead analyzed the accepted principles to which plantiffs and defendants referred in arguing their cases. Because arguments in court must refer to accepted practices in order to be convincing, it is the justificatory argument that reveals shared norms and intersubjectivity. Writes Cohen,

> Although interpreting litigators' assumptions (like selecting and compiling numerical data) involves some subjectivity, the validity of the conclusions drawn from forensic attestation can be tested directly and independently: one need only read the texts cited. Generalizations based on cliometric analysis can be challenged only if the reader has the time and expertise to compile all the data anew (which of course rarely happens), or if (as here) the statistical conclusions directly contradict the premises clearly underlying arguments being made by Athenian litigants.[1]

By examining how policy makers defined the situation, we can understand why they chose certain responses to the challenge of petrodollar recycling. By reviewing how they justified those responses, we are able to identify the shared understandings of legitimacy to which they resorted.

As I hope I have made clear, this analysis is not itself subjective. I do

[1] Cohen, *Athenian Economy.*

not subscribe to the view that all interpretation and argumentation is necessarily subjective. Intersubjective understandings, though difficult to identify in a rigorous fashion, exist in objective reality. In this analysis I attempt to present objective observation and interpretation of inter-subjective phenomena.

SOCIAL PURPOSE AND POLITICAL CONTEXT

Balance-of-Payments Adjustment Financing under Bretton Woods

A necessary precondition for the smooth functioning of international financial markets is the provision (by a hegemonic power) of the three goals of an international monetary order: confidence, liquidity, and a balance-of-payments adjustment mechanism.[2]

The Bretton Woods system, which codified social purpose among the advanced industrialized democracies after World War II, provided for balance-of-payments adjustment financing through the International Monetary Fund. It was a system based on fixed exchange rates, which meant that if a nation ran a trade deficit it did not have the option of adjusting by devaluating the exchange rate. Nations denied recourse to international financial institutions had either to restrict demand (dampening the desire for imports and lowering the price of exports) or to raise interest rates (to attract foreign capital). Either policy would have the effect of slowing down the economy and putting people out of work. Political leaders, when faced with the choice of causing a recession or breaking the rules of the monetary system and devaluing, were not likely to choose the Bretton Woods agreement. Their careers, and indeed their democratic responsibilities as elected representatives, depended on sacrificing the objectives of the international monetary system in favor of domestic welfare concerns. To make the choice easier on national leaders, the Bretton Woods system allowed for very gradual adjustment in the balance of payments by giving leaders access to capital.

Although the Bretton Woods system was meant to institutionalize the ideals of international liberalism, free markets were a rarity. States retained strict controls over the movement of money into and out of their borders. This practice stemmed not only from the practical realities of a world recovering from war but also from the social purpose that these institutional elements of the financial system embodied.

[2] Cohen, *Organizing the World's Money.*

The main theme in the social purpose promulgated by the United States was the compromise of embedded liberalism—the international liberalism of strong states embedded in the historical development of the nation-state.[3] Given sovereignty and the right to noninterference in domestic affairs, the nation-state system is fundamentally at odds with the idea of laissez-faire international markets. In part, embedded liberalism represents a compromise between the ideology of open and free international markets, which came to fruition in the nineteenth century, and the right of the nation-state to protect its domestic society from interference against national welfare objectives. Embedded liberalism also stemmed from the need to regulate markets and was a reaction to the burgeoning of market forces before World War II. The Great Depression brought home the brutality that unregulated markets could wreak on unprotected domestic markets.[4]

This theme of social purpose served as an important prelude to the problem of recycling in the 1970s. Balance-of-payments adjustment financing was provided by international financial institutions as a prerequisite to cooperation by nations and to assure that they would abide by the rules of the system. Markets were not given much of a role in balance-of-payments financing, but they took on the brunt of responsibility after the collapse of the Bretton Woods system in 1971. Without the resources to continue its role, the primary provider of balance-of-payments finance began to shift from the IMF to international capital markets. Markets were assigned the role of providing efficient outcomes, so long as prices did not fluctuate too rapidly.

Bretton Woods was certainly not a perfect system of international monetary order, and it would have been hard-pressed to cope with a shock such as petrodollar recycling. Indeed, whenever there was a shock to the international monetary system or symptoms of severe pressure on it, advanced industrialized democracies cooperated on an ad hoc basis. The two tier arrangement in response to turmoil in international gold markets is an example.

Yet by the same token, nations had at least some idea of what to expect under the Bretton Woods system. The oil price shock of 1973–74 challenged international monetary cooperation just as the rules of the monetary regime collapsed. Principles of allocation were not entirely explicit, and national policy makers were unsure of what precisely to expect.

[3] Ruggie, "International Regimes."
[4] Polanyi, *Great Transformation.*

The Political Background to the Recycling Problem

It was already clear that uncertainty, monetary chaos, and leadership vacuums would characterize the year 1973 long before consumers of petrol had to wait in line. Nixon had just begun to defend himself against accusations of complicity in the Watergate break-in, and the highly centralized executive branch that he had until then run from his office was, at least for matters of economic policy, left in disarray. In France, Georges Pompidou was in his last year of presidency and his ill health precluded him from vigorous policy making. Britain's Labour Party was about to cede government to the Tories for the longest period in this century, and the leading parties in Germany and Japan had likewise lost popular support.

Economically, 1973 marked a transition from the closing of the gold window and the breakdown of the Bretton Woods system to a new system of ad hoc arrangements and dirty floats.[5] World inflation reached postwar highs as European welfare-state policies began to overtake growth, and U.S. spending on Vietnam continued to leave a dollar overhang that hurt confidence in American ability to provide the world with a key currency. The early 1970s also witnessed massive crop failures and an increased maldistribution in the global balance of payments. In short, the world economy was in shambles, and there was no leadership in the leading nation states to cope with it.

By 1975, however, the leadership in Western industrial countries was at an all-time high for support and stability. Gerald Ford decentralized the executive branch and attempted to heal the national wounds of Watergate. Valéry Giscard d'Estaing once again demonstrated the efficacy of the state in France. Helmut Schmidt had replaced the scandalized Willy Brandt, and Edward Heath's government was replaced by a Conservative party that would not countenance striking coal miners. Japan also enjoyed new leadership. As George de Menil notes, d'Estaing was to be president for seven years and Schmidt the chancellor for eight. A combination of personal authority and constitutional mandate was to secure for each man a longer term of office than that enjoyed by any other leader of the major industrial democracies during the decade.[6] The time was ripe for economic cooperation between the advanced industrialized democracies.

---

[5] A *dirty float* is an exchange rate that ostensibly is left to market forces but in which government institutions intercede to affect market outcomes.

[6] De Menil and Solomon, *Economic Summitry*, pp. 12–13.

With the collapse of the Bretton Woods system came an increased need for international cooperation, particularly by the advanced industrialized economies. Academic researchers trace international policy coordination back to the response of industrialized countries to the oil shock and to petrodollar recycling.[7] In one of the first scholarly monographs to explore the phenomenon of economic summitry, George de Menil and Anthony M. Solomon describe cooperation to form an oil consumers' regime as a precursor to international economic policy coordination.[8] A detailed examination of events of the mid-1970s does indeed show that relations among the advanced industrialized economies in response to the first oil shock were a harbinger of the nature of their economic relations in later years. North-north relations were autarkic and uncooperative. The U.S. response to the rise of oil prices in the mid-1970s was an attempt to reassert its dominance in the global economy.

Oil prices rose in the 1970s because market conditions and the changing structure of the oil industry enabled producing states to wrest control of production from transnational corporations. Host countries had faced an oligopsony of companies buying crude petroleum.[9] Those companies, dominated by the Seven Sisters, colluded to limit oil production and to suppress the price they paid for crude in order to maximize profits at the gasoline pumps, which they owned.[10]

Oil prices rose for two reasons. First, and most important, was the sharp secular rise in demand for petroleum products after World War II as world industry grew and became reliant on energy from fossil fuels. A second important factor, too often overlooked in analyses of OPEC, was the introduction of independent oil companies into the world oil industry. These independents broke the oligopsony power of the Seven Sisters, or at least were a sign and symptom of the end of collusion among the major petroleum-buying firms.

OPEC members neither grabbed control of their oil nor raised its price so much as the majors lost control and ceased in their ability to artificially suppress prices. Before the 1970s, any oil-producing state

[7] See, for example, de Menil, "De Rambouillet à Versailles." To a lesser extent this view is also expressed in Putnam and Bayne, *Hanging Together*, chap. 2.

[8] De Menil and Solomon, *Economic Summitry*.

[9] An oligopsony is to buyers what an oligopoly is to sellers. If there are only a few buyers in the market, they can collude to keep the price of a commodity low.

[10] Enrico Mattei, who was head of the Italian oil company ENI, is credited with calling the oligopsony of oil companies *Sette Sorrelle*, or Seven Sisters. They were Standard Oil of New Jersey (Exxon), Standard Oil of New York (Mobil), Standard Oil of California (Chevron), Texaco, Gulf, Shell, and BP. Yergin, *The Prize*, p. 503.

that tried to take control of its own resources was quickly shut out of the oil export market by an effective boycott of its product by the major firms. Two important examples were Mexico (which went from the world's second largest exporter of petroleum to a net importer of petroleum products after it nationalized oil company assets in 1938) and Iran (whose popularly elected Prime Minister was overthrown in a coup sponsored by the Central Intelligence Agency [CIA] after he nationalized oil company assets in 1953). Oil producers saw that the winds of control had changed direction after Algeria and Libya both successfully renegotiated the terms of concession agreements with the independents in 1970 and 1971. By 1973 the largest oil companies in the capitalist world had gathered at Teheran voluntarily to rewrite the profit sharing and equity terms of the concessions with OPEC members.[11]

In the autumn of 1973, the oil shock was perceived as being linked tightly to the Arab-Israeli war. The rise in oil prices was therefore falsely ascribed to a new political efficacy of Arab states and was seen as a hostile act toward the Western alliance. Because the war was the responsibility of the State Department, because Secretary of State Kissinger enjoyed such dominance over the foreign policy making apparatus of the United States, and because much of the response to the oil shock involved attempts at coordination with allies in Europe—and policy coordination was then the realm of the Department of State—much of the initial policy was formulated by Henry Kissinger.

Kissinger's strategy was threefold. First, because he thought that the the Arab-Israeli conflict was the proximate cause of the oil price rise, Kissinger worked hard at shuttle diplomacy to bring a cease-fire and then a framework for a peace settlement to the Middle East. He found, however, that there was little correlation between peace in the Middle East and moderation in oil prices.[12] It is clear, both from his memoirs

[11] For the history of this period, see al-Otaiba, *OPEC*; Tétreault, *Revolution in the World Petroleum Market*; and Yergin, *Prize*. On the Algerian negotiations see Doucy and Monheim, "La Révolution."

[12] In later congressional testimony, the chief engineer for Aramco argued that the cutback in Saudi oil production had been necessitated by the threat of a dome collapse in the Shedgum section of the Ghawar field—one of the largest oil fields in the world. Unless production in this field was halted and seawater was pumped in to repressurize it, Aramco would permanently damage one of the world's largest known reserves of petroleum. If this is so, then Kissinger's attempt at shuttle diplomacy could have had little effect on oil prices. See Testimony of the Chief Reservoir Engineer of Socal before the Church Committee, cited in Achnacarry, "Petroleum Crisis," p. 3. For monthly production figures, see Central Intelligence Agency, *Journal of Energy Statistics*, various issues.

and from his statements at the time, that Kissinger soon delinked the issues of the Arab-Israeli conflict and OPEC's official crude pricing.[13]

Not surprisingly, given Kissinger's worldview and style of diplomacy, his second set of responses consisted of carrots and sticks. The sticks were ominous statements that implicitly threatened a boycott of OPEC members by food exporters. For example, in the opening paragraph of a statement to the press on the energy policy of the United States in January 1974, Kissinger warned that "the energy crisis reflects a basic problem for the entire international community for the foreseeable future that today concerns energy but that in the future may concern other raw materials or foodstuffs where incentives for supply are out of proportion to the demand."[14] Asked by the press to elaborate, Kissinger added that "we saw temporarily some pressure on the food situation last year. It behooves all nations to take a look at their long-term problems so that we can deal thoughtfully with them before they become acute."[15]

Another stick was the threat of energy self-sufficiency and the development of alternative energy schemes. This was a very real threat to OPEC (especially to those producers with large reserves, such as Saudi Arabia) because it not only ruined the present market for their exports and whatever leverage those exports obtained but also threatened to destroy all future demand for oil. Along with these very severe threats, Kissinger offered the carrots of friendly relations and investment funds for OPEC capital surpluses. The investment fund was simply offered by Kissinger as an idea—it never got further than very preliminary statements, and indeed the need for it was obviated as Eurodollar banks recovered from the collapses of Herstatt and Franklin National and began to take large deposits.

Both the threat of developing an alternative energy supply and the incentive of an investment fund were based on the economic theory of exhaustible resources developed by Harold Hotelling in 1931 and extended by William Nordhaus in 1973. Hotelling compared the mining of minerals to clipping coupons on a bond. An investor has the choice

[13] Kissinger said at a press conference that "no [oil] producing nation has linked its response to a further evolution of the Arab-Israeli negotiations. And we believe that this linkage would be irrelevant to the basic problem." Department of State, *Bulletin* 70, no. 1806, 14 February 1974; p. 117 (transcript of press conference held on 10 January 1974 in Washington, D.C.). It is, of course, likely that this statement was rhetoric and more true than Kissinger knew at the time.

[14] Department of State, *Bulletin* 70, no. 1806, 14 February 1974; 109.

[15] Ibid., p. 114. The states in the Arab Peninsula reacted to this threat by planning a $9-billion "breadbasket of the Middle East" in the Sudan. This plan was strongly disapproved of by Western donors and never came to fruition. See "The Sudan from Bread Basket to Basket Case" in Spiro, *Policy Coordination*, chap. 11.

of keeping a bond, which provides certain income in the future, or selling it, which provides cash in the present. Whether the investor keeps the bond or sells it depends on the present value of discounted future capital. If investing $1,000 today would give a 5 percent return for the next ten years, then she will keep a $1,000 bond only if it promises to give more than 5 percent over ten years.[16] Similarly, an OPEC country would produce oil only if cash gained from the sale today is worth more in ten years than oil left in the ground for ten years. Thus, to encourage oil production, Kissinger tried to convince OPEC members that the value of cash would rise faster than the value of unlifted oil.

A variant of this strategy was the threat of alternative energy sources. The threat comes at what Nordhaus calls the switchpoint to a backstop technology. In English, this means that when oil reaches a certain price it is economically viable to research and manufacture synthetic fuels (or similar substitutes for oil such as better batteries for electrically driven cars). At this point, increasing demand for energy and decreasing supply of oil do not lead to rises in the price of oil. And because the price trajectory of oil reaches a plateau, the present discounted price for future sales of oil decreases. Given the possibility of alternative energy sources in the future, oil sold now will result in cash that increases in value faster than oil not sold now.[17] Thus both the threat to develop alternative energy sources and the plan to offer an investment fund to OPEC states were implicit means to decrease the value of OPEC's oil reserves. Consideration of Arab investment was entirely within the framework of lower oil prices.

Kissinger's third category of response to the oil shock was to turn to oil-consuming nations in Europe to coordinate policy. This coordination involved a hypothetical buyers' cartel (the reestablishment of an oligopsony that would be explicitly controlled by states rather than by firms as in the past) and also collective management of the current account deficits that were accruing to oil producers.[18] The object of cooperation was to lower artificially the price of oil, with balance-of-payments financing as an ancillary component.

In sum, the political background to petrodollar recycling was characterized by State Department policies oriented toward the short term and toward lowering the price of oil. Because the problem was seen as

[16] Hotelling, "Economics of Exhaustible Resources."

[17] Nordhaus, "Allocation of Energy Resources." An earlier critique of Hotelling's assumptions on exhaustion points is in Gordon, "Reinterpretation." See also Heal, "Relationship between Price and Extraction Cost."

[18] Kapstein, *Insecure Alliance.*

temporary, Kissinger attempted to bring down market prices rather than face issues of balance-of-payments adjustment financing. These policies were harbingers of the politics of petrodollar recycling because they embodied the same set of relationships between international markets and international authority. Market outcomes were considered to be outside of the realm of legitimate state response to the oil shock. Cooperation meant collusion among the advanced industrialized democracies to fix the price of oil. Bidding for petroleum on international markets was considered to be defection. Letting markets work was not a part of international policy coordination. These same themes were to be applied later to capital markets for petrodollars.

DEFINING THE PROBLEM

Recycling was not important to policy makers immediately after the oil price shock of 1973–74. They worried primarily about the economic effects of higher oil prices and the problem of securing a steady and reliable supply of foreign petroleum. American officials maintained the belief that oil prices would eventually return to "normal." Recycling was considered to be a short-term strategy to provide attractive investments for oil producers. Those making policy believed that persistent balance-of-payments imbalances were avoidable. To the extent that recycling was seen as a problem, it was overshadowed by a multitude of more immediate concerns.

Early definitions of the threat to the international monetary order posed by the first oil shock and the need to recycle the surplus of oil producers to the deficits of oil consumers focused on the possibility of trade wars and beggar-thy-neighbor policies, the strain on the international banking system, the vulnerability of the West to financial blackmail by OPEC, and the general dangers posed by uneven international distribution of current account deficits and surpluses. Definitions varied slightly from State to Treasury to the Fed, each according to the individual portfolio of the department, but none were mutually exclusive or contradictory. All agreed on the danger of unilateral adjustment, just as all agreed on the ability of the United States to pursue its own interest to the detriment of the international system, if need be.

Recycling as a Prisoners' Dilemma

During the Nixon and Ford administrations, American policy makers viewed the problem posed by the rise in the price of crude petroleum as analogous to the situation that had led to the Great Depression. Markets would not automatically provide stability, efficient allocation of resources, or harmony of interests. If each nation acted in its own interest, the outcome would be to the detriment of all nations. In the language of game theory, this was a single-play Prisoners' Dilemma. Although policy makers did not use the jargon of game theory, former academics such as Kissinger and Shultz clearly were informed by an understanding of sub-Pareto optimal Nash equilibria.[19]

Kissinger viewed state participation in markets as a sort of defection (in the game of Prisoners' Dilemma) because the economies of advanced industrialized democracies would suffer if they did not collude against OPEC. "The only result of unmanaged bilateralism will be to bid up prices," Kissinger told Organization for Economic Cooperation and Development (OECD) ministers of finance, and that would "ruin the countries making the bilateral arrangements before they ruin everyone else." In the absence of a cooperative solution, each nation would face the temptation to shift its problems onto others. "This was the approach the industrial world followed during the 'beggar-thy-neighbor' policies of the 1930's," Kissinger warned. "We all know the consequences." Because cooperation represented much more than immediate economic stability, the challenge of how nations responded to the oil shock was, according to Kissinger a test of "the fragile fabric of international principles and institutions."[20] Failure to cooperate "would threaten the world with a vicious cycle of competition, autarky, rivalry, and depression such as led to the collapse of the world order in the thirties."[21]

William Casey, whose apparent skill at effecting transnational capital flows came to light much later, was under secretary of state for economic affairs in 1974. He noted that "the dilemma faced by each [oil] consumer country is how to generate sufficient foreign exchange to pay its increased oil import bill without cutting down on non-oil imports."[22] Unless the capital surplus of oil producers flowed back to consuming nations so as to permit "reasonable growth," those countries would experience reductions in employment and output.

If nations did attempt to bring their trade accounts into balance, the

[19] A Pareto optimum is the combination of strategies for which neither player can achieve a better payoff without making the other accept a worse payoff. At the Nash equilibrium neither player has an incentive to switch strategies.

[20] Department of State, *Bulletin* 70, no. 1810, 4 March 1974; 203.

[21] Ibid., p. 201.

[22] William Casey, "International Economic Affairs in 1974 [a speech made before the Public Affairs Council at Washington on 28 February (press release 75)]," reprinted in Department of State *Bulletin* 70, no. 1813, 25 March 1974; p. 304.

result would be "unrestricted bilateral competition," according to Kissinger, and that would "be ruinous for all of the countries concerned." The short-term benefits to each defecting nation-state "will be at the cost of world stability and of the world economy."[23] It was senseless for advanced industrial economies even to attempt adjustment because "no conceivable increase in bilateral trade with the producing nations can cover the massive payments deficits that each nation faces."[24]

As Casey had pointed out, nations would face less of an incentive to bring their trade accounts into balance if they had access to capital. Yet this presented an additional collective action dilemma because nations also had an incentive to draw in as much capital as possible. Putting both the capital and trade incentives into the framework of a Prisoners' Dilemma, Casey said:

> Such measures as exchange rate depreciation, import restriction, export subsidation, controls on capital outflow, and interest rate or other incentives to encourage capital inflow are of little use in the present situation because the terms of trade have shifted against all oil-importing countries simultaneously. Use of any of these tools by individual nations would quickly be frustrated by similar actions on the part of their trading partners. This could lead to a competitive wave of restrictive measures or bidding for capital that would risk a serious drop in world trade, a deflationary downspiral, and possibly worldwide depression.[25]

At a news conference with Simon (then administrator of the Federal Energy Office), Kissinger observed that the United States was "well placed in this competition" and had "the capability to withstand it better than any potential competitor." Response to the oil shock, however, had to be solved "on a common basis if we are not going to suffer very severe consequences for international stability and for the international economy."[26] When asked what might happen if countries did make bilateral agreements with OPEC, as France had begun to do shortly beforehand, Kissinger warned: "The conditions which I described of unrestricted competition cannot be avoided by unilateral efforts. And therefore the challenge to the statesmanship of all of the consuming na-

[23] Department of State, *Bulletin* 70, no. 1806, 14 February 1974; p. 110.
[24] Department of State, *Bulletin* 70, no. 1810, 4 March 1974; p. 203.
[25] Casey, "International Economic Affairs." Department of State *Bulletin* 70, no. 1813, 25 March 1974.
[26] Department of State, *Bulletin* 70, no. 1806, 14 February 1974; p. 110.

tions is whether they are able to recognize this fact—because if not, reality will impose it on them."[27]

After warning against beggar-thy-neighbor policies, Shultz called on OECD nations "to resist those pressures for the introduction of special-interest-serving government . . . interventions which are likely to be put forward during any time of rapid economic change."[28] What he did not say publicly was that the largest special-interest-serving government intervention was likely to come from the United States. As Kissinger had pointed out, the United States was in a dominant position to attract Arab capital, and it had a very real incentive to do so. Despite his warning on the dangers of competing unilaterally for foreign capital, Casey advocated attracting funds from abroad. "We will have to make securities an export," he announced in a State Department press release. "We will have to maintain and strengthen our ability to raise capital throughout the world as well as at home."[29]

The implication of defining the situation as a Prisoners' Dilemma was that policy makers realized the strong reasons for the United States to defect. Simon simply could not stop worrying about the federal demand on capital markets, and he put forward this problem most forcefully at the start of 1975:

> In order to meet Federal borrowing needs, we now anticipate that during the calendar year 1975, the Treasury Department will be coming into the capital markets for almost $70 billion of net new financing. . . . On top of this immense total, federally sponsored agencies—FNMA, Federal Home Loan Banks, the Farm Credit Agencies, and others—may account for another $10 billion in borrowing. As a result, the Federal Government will be raising more net new money in the capital markets than was raised by all borrowers combined—public and private—last year, or in any other year in the past.
>
> The strains could be relieved if the . . . OPEC nations put a larger amount of their accumulated funds into investment in this country, or if the American public spends less and saves more.[30]

[27] Ibid., p. 116.
[28] Statement by Treasury Secretary Shultz before the Washington Energy Conference, 11 February 1974, reprinted in Department of State *Bulletin* 70, no. 1810, 4 March 1974; p. 217.
[29] Casey, "International Economic Affairs," Department of State, *Bulletin* 70, no. 1813, 25 March 1974; p. 307.
[30] U.S. Congress, Senate, Committee on Finance, *Effect of Petrodollars*, pp. 11–12.

Given his options of competing for OPEC capital or having to convince the American public to spend less and save more, it is easy to understand why Simon chose the former.

By defining the situation as a Prisoners' Dilemma, U.S. policy makers implicitly argued that markets could not solve the challenge of petrodollar recycling in an optimal fashion. They defined the legitimate response to the oil shock in terms of collusion among the advanced industrialized nations. Because collusion does not sound very nice, they referred to it as international cooperation. Because of the Prisoners' Dilemma dynamic, cooperation was necessary for the efficient and optimal allocation of value. A solution involving political distribution of oil and capital meant that value was to be allocated by authoritative means. Leaving outcomes to markets, which would have meant a suboptimal solution, was seen as illegitimate.

It is important to realize that policy makers saw the world as a single-play Prisoners' Dilemma, with the logical implication that authoritative arrangements were necessary for cooperation. No policy maker viewed the problem as a game with repeated plays or as an iterated Prisoners' Dilemma. The notion of reciprocity was recognized only insofar as it would lead to a downward spiral of retaliatory defection. The possibility of cooperation through iterated "tit-for-tat" strategies was not perceived by any of the statespeople concerned with the oil shock, not even those who had come to their positions by way of the academy. Cooperation through an iterated Prisoners' Dilemma with "tit-for-tat" strategies was not a part of the policy discourse.

It is also important to note that policy makers viewed the world as consisting primarily of advanced industrialized economies. It does not seem to have occurred to them that the result of their defection in the Prisoners' Dilemma might be to shift all of the negative consequences of defection to LDCs. If there was a trade deficit that all had to share, and if they competed to adjust their trade balances, the structural deficit would have shifted to weaker nations. Though this outcome was not explicitly envisioned, it surely would have been perceived as illegitimate.

Markets and Political Authority

By the time of the first oil shock, international capital markets were far from staunch and secure. Two of the largest banks in the world, Franklin National and Herstatt, had closed their doors in 1974 in the middle of a business day, leaving payments to the clearinghouses of international markets up to their receivers.[31] These and seven other bank failures in one fiscal year had lowered confidence in the interbank market dramatically. In a private conversation with officials of the Treasury Department, an official of the Foreign Department of the New York Federal Reserve Bank was alarmed that the volume of international transactions handled through New York had averaged $65 billion each day before the Herstatt failure and was down to less than half that by the end of July 1974. The bankers' acceptance market had "dried up," he said, and smaller banks were unable to place acceptances in the interbank market. In a memorandum of conversation written by the Treasury officials, the central banker is reported to have said:

> Ever since the failure of Bankhaus I. D. Herstatt on June 26 there has been a possibility of panic; he felt that all the ingredients for financial chaos were there. . . .
> The New York Fed, he said, was placing bank rescue at the top of its priorities, as was the Bank of England.[32]

The instability of the interbank market meant that there was no guarantee that the banks with the lion's share of OPEC money would redistribute those funds to other banks that needed short-term money. The result would have been one set of banks that did not wish to accept OPEC money and another set of banks that would have had to call in loans. The interbank market prevents this imbalance of assets and liabilities, and in this sense it acts as an intermediary between borrowers and lenders. In the mid-1970s, however, the market sometimes failed to serve this function. Some banks reportedly offered negative interest rates on OPEC capital.

Without an efficient interbank market, it was more vital than ever that banks balance the maturity distribution of liabilities and assets within their own organizations. As an example, Bankers' Trust might accept deposits from Qatar on an overnight basis (Qatar had the option of withdrawing its money every twenty-four hours), but it might lend funds to Uruguay for six months. If Qatar did, in fact, withdraw its money instead of rolling over the deposit, the bank would be strapped for cash. At the very least Bankers' Trust would have uncovered interest rate risk, and even that risk rested on a functioning interbank market. The instability of the interbank market in 1974 was, therefore, a cause for ex-

[31] Spero, *Failure of Franklin National.*
[32] Keyser to Willett.

treme concern to bankers, particularly because of the imbalance in the maturity distribution of OPEC deposits and loans to oil importers. One banker told an interviewer from the Federal Reserve Board: "The banks in the market will have an increasing concern with their liquidity as their deposits from only a few large depositors tend to build up very rapidly, and in comparatively liquid forms. It would be expected that before long the banks would be under considerable pressure to accept those funds only in terms of longer term deposits with no take-out provisions."[33]

Later in the year, a senior vice-president in charge of the international division at a large New York bank told Treasury officials that Arab governments were insisting on "call money" (money that can be withdrawn in under seven days) despite the fact that most banks were offering interest rates well below those they offered other depositors. "Seven days nothing," the *New York Times* quoted a London banker as saying, "we wish we could hold the money for more than 24 hours."[34]

The concern that markets would not work began to reflect an implicit assumption that a major function of financial intermediation is to bridge the gap between depositors who desire liquidity and borrowers who wish for the security of a long-term loan. This definition of the problem soon spread to the Department of State, as was attested to by Alfred Atherton, the assistant secretary of state for Near Eastern and South Asian Affairs:

> [The Eurocurrency] market is showing signs of substantial strain. Banks are finding it increasingly burdensome to intermediate between their rapidly growing short-term deposit liabilities and the longer term financial needs of oil importers. Their capital-liability ratios are being altered, and they are concerned about the implications for bank liquidity of potential withdrawal of a few large depositors.[35]

In the logic of how policy makers defined the situation, this problem was not caused by the oil shock or by any actions that OPEC took. Instead, the root cause was the instability of international capital markets and the vulnerability of those markets to the economically rational actions of depositors. An illustration of this vulnerability was the potential

[33] Pizer to Bryant. It is not clear which banks were interviewed because although the document was not declassified, the bankers' names were whited out.

[34] "Rising Oil Prices Creating Dismay," *New York Times*, 17 June 1974.

[35] Testimony of Alfred L. Atherton Jr., U.S. Congress, House, Committee on Foreign Affairs, *U.S.-Europe Relations.*

for extreme fluctuations in the U.S. money supply caused by the loss of confidence in the interbank market in 1974. A hypothetical example might be an oil company based in Texas that had to pay Saudi Arabia for crude petroleum imports. The company might have had an account with First Texas Bank, and to pay Saudi Arabia it would withdraw money from its First Texas account and send it to the Saudi account at Morgan Guaranty. The Federal Reserve System permits banks in the United States to lend out a certain percentage of their deposits, and the percentage that they are not allowed to lend out is called the "reserve requirement." Now let us imagine that First Texas had lent out less than it was permitted, and Morgan Guaranty was "loaned up" (in the jargon of the Fed), which means that it could not issue more loans until it received more deposit money. The effect of a withdrawal from First Texas would not change the money supply in the United States because loss of deposit money would not require it to call in loans. Additional deposits with Morgan Guaranty, however, would create credit because it could issue new loans with the new money in the account it held for the Saudis. Thus the simple transfer of $1 billion from one American bank to another might raise the money supply (depending on the credit multiplier) by many billions. The reverse was also seen as possible by the Fed; if money went from a loaned-up bank to one that could still lend money and preserve its reserve ratio, then a drastic fall in the money supply would ensue.

Deposits that were moved from U.S. banks to markets abroad could also cause rapid swings in the domestic money supply. At least one New York banker told Treasury officials that if Arab central banks shifted deposits from domestic branches to the Eurodollar market, the result would be deflationary.

> [The Treasury officials] pointed out to him that the Arabs were being paid in New York deposits, and their ownership of these deposits did not really remove them from the U.S. money supply. Mr. [deleted] seemed unable to grasp this point, and insisted that the Arabs' deposits in the London branches were subject to British regulation, should any regulation be adopted, and belonged in London; they could not be pulled back to New York at the whim of the parent banks.[36]

But if Treasury officials insisted on giving international bankers lessons in free market economics, the Federal Reserve Board had more

---

[36] Willett to Bennett.

sympathy. In a statement sent to a Senate committee, the Fed warned, "Banks are limited in the volume of deposits they can safely accept by the need to maintain an appropriate relationship between their capital accounts and their over-all liabilities or assets. . . . Appropriate fiscal and monetary policies should be able to maintain a high level of economic activity regardless of whether foreigners acquire assets in our country or not."[37] But, of course, the ability of "appropriate fiscal and monetary policies" to smooth out monetary aggregates depended on the Fed's ability to observe and measure the flows of funds in the United States.

Control of the money supply was not yet a target of the Fed in 1974, but the vice-president of the Foreign Department of the New York Fed in 1974 recalled his goal as "control (by off-setting operations) of the amounts [of OPEC funds] coming in."[38] If the funds coming into U.S. capital markets were visible to the Fed, the Fed would be able to control their impact on market stability. "We wanted the dollars moving through channels where you could see it," explained another New York Fed vice-president. "We not just wanted the money in the U.S., but wanted to lock it up."[39]

Another concern was the potential for interest rate differentials between capital markets to increase. A member of the Board of Governors of the Fed testified in August 1974 that if OPEC governments invested funds that were liquid, short-term, and backed by strong guarantees, "That would imply some shifts in the yields on different kinds of financial assets in national markets, reducing yields on more liquid assets relative to yields on, say, mortgages. In the case of the United States, if there should be a large inflow to major U.S. banks and to treasury obligations, as seems possible, some downward pressure may result on yields in those sectors."[40] During the same month, Fed chairman Arthur Burns observed, "Clearly, the American economy is not being starved for funds. On the contrary, growth of money and credit is still proceeding at a faster rate than is consistent with general price stability over the longer term." He also remarked the "tension in international financial markets" and consumer interest rates "such as we have not previously known in over a century of our Nation's recorded experience."[41]

The concern by bankers that markets were not working extended to

---

[37] Federal Reserve *Bulletin*, November 1974, pp. 759 and 761.

[38] Interview with Richard Debs, New York, 14 September 1983.

[39] Interview with Jeffrey Shafer, Washington, D.C., 16 September 1983.

[40] Statement by Henry C. Wallich, U.S. Congress, House, Committee on Banking and Currency, *International Petrodollar Crisis*, reprinted in Federal Reserve *Bulletin*, July 1974, p. 573.

[41] Statement by Arthur Burns before the Joint Economic Committee of the U.S. Congress, Federal Reserve *Bulletin*, July 1974, p. 564.

the area of bank failures. Even after the initial panic in 1974 had died down and banks had time for careful retrospection, they supported an active statement from the international community that someone somewhere would be a lender of last resort. In the absence of such international action, one banker testified to Congress,

> intergovernmental support would be of a much more ad-hoc nature and the danger of a breakdown of the international financial system would be greater. If private financial institutions were forced to cease operations in certain countries, owing to a lack of adequate safeguards, the most probable result would be a resort to conflict provoking initiatives. Unilateral restrictions on imports have already been imposed.[42]

Bankers, in short, feared that markets would not function automatically, and they wanted a political solution. They knew better than others that there was no inherent reason for recycling to take place automatically through international capital markets. On the liability side of their balance sheets, banking officials feared the short-term nature of Arab deposits, and they saw no reason that those deposits would necessarily continue (or stay in their banks). On the asset side, they feared reaching the prudent limits of credit exposure to any one borrower, and they did not like lending for periods that were substantially longer than the maturity distribution of the deposit base. Bankers told officials from the Federal Reserve System and from the Treasury that they felt recycling was the proper domain of the government. For the senior vice president at a major New York money center, the solution was "U.S. government action, and he indicated that he felt that Secretary Simon understood this point and was taking appropriate action in his visit to the Middle East. Treasury Specials would be in order, as would multilateral international institutions."[43] His suggestion, in other words, was that recycling would not be automatic, and the government should take the responsibility of being an international financial intermediary. The stage was set for the U.S. government to take responsibility for petrodollar recycling.

North-South Relations

A third element of policy makers' definition of the situation was the effect of recycling (or lack of it) on North-South relations. Kissinger

[42] Statement of William A. Hurst, Vice-President, Bank of America, U.S. Congress, Senate, Committee on Banking Housing and Urban Affairs, *Financial Support Fund.*
[43] Willett to Bennett.

pointed out in November 1974 that while OPEC revenues would inevitably flow back to the consumer nations, "they will not necessarily flow back to the countries whose balance of payments is most acute."[44] At a meeting of the Ministerial Council of the OECD, the U.S. special ambassador for trade negotiations, William Eberle, summed up the problem as ensuring "an adequate transfer of resources to those developing countries whose need has been most seriously aggravated by the high price of oil."[45]

Eberle noted that by definition financial flows from OPEC had to equal the deficit of the consuming nations. He defined the problem as one of distributing the capital flows from OPEC. "The OECD countries and the stronger developing countries can probably rely primarily on the private markets to distribute capital, although it is clear that international institutions and governments should stand ready with a safety net. Governmental policies will play an important role in determining how well the private markets fulfill this task."[46]

A Fed official also made public his doubt that private markets could recycle petrodollars from surplus countries to those with deficits: "The term 'recycling' is appropriate, if at all, only in the sense that the OPEC countries cannot avoid placing their surplus funds somewhere—but it tends to obscure the fact that the financing of deficits of particular oil importers is far from automatic."[47]

Although the plight of LDC oil importers was a concern to U.S. policy makers, an equally vital area of anxiety was the threat that OPEC might politically manipulate financial markets. The Arab members of OPEC, after all, had just declared an oil embargo on the United States. It was not entirely unreasonable to assume that a country such as Saudi Arabia might use its economic position against the West again, causing financial havoc by using its investments as a political weapon. OECD countries, according to Kissinger, "all will be vulnerable to massive sudden withdrawals."

[44] Address by Henry Kissinger to the University of Chicago Board of Trustees, Chicago, 14 November 1974, reprinted in Department of State *Bulletin* 71, no. 1849, 2 December 1974; p. 753.

[45] Statement of William D. Eberle, Ministerial Council of the OECD, Paris, 29 May 1974, reprinted in Department of State *Bulletin* 71, no. 1827, 1 July 1974; pp. 25–26.

[46] Ibid.

[47] "Statement to Congress," 16 October 1974, reprinted in the Federal Reserve *Bulletin*, November 1974, p. 759.

Consumers [cannot] finance their oil bill by going into debt to the producers without making their domestic structure hostage to the decisions
of others. Already, producers have the power to cause major financial
upheavals simply by shifting investment funds from one country to another or even from one institution to another. The political implications
are ominous and unpredictable. Those who wield financial power would
sooner or later seek to dictate the political terms of the new relationships.[48]

This risk of "exaggerated" movements in markets was a problem for
bankers as well as for the Fed. Price swings might have resulted if OPEC
members were to shift their funds between banks or between currencies.[49] Even if such moves were motivated by a simple desire to diversify
portfolios, a New York Fed report said, "the diversification process
could feed on itself, driving exchange rates to levels unjustified by
trade or general economic performance."[50] The concern was brought
about by widespread rumors of OPEC diversification and by the fact
that the New York Fed itself had recently sold nearly $100 million for
purchases of Deutsche marks on behalf of foreign central banks. One
Arab country was reported to have affected the market when it shifted
out of sterling and into Deutsche marks, and another Arab central
bank "suddenly dumped more than $250 million on the market on
October 9."[51]
In response to perceptions of this problem, the Treasury did several
studies on the effects of sudden shifts in OPEC funds. The first of the
studies came out in the summer of 1974, and it explained, in essence,
that so long as everything neo-classical economists assume held true
there could not be chaos in financial markets. The report assumed, for
instance, that Arab investors would make purely rational decisions
about their investments (i.e., not use investments for political leverage)
and that they would pursue "rational" (as defined by Treasury economists) portfolio diversification strategies from the beginning of their
capital accumulation. But these authors knew that Arab states lacked
the technical capacity to diversify such a large and sudden portfolio
from the very moment those states began to accumulate capital sur-

---

[48] Address by Henry Kissinger, Department of State *Bulletin* 71, no. 1984, p. 750.
[49] An example is Statement of William A. Hurst. *Financial Support Fund.*
[50] Pardee to Coombs, 28 October 1974. The memo was forwarded to Arthur Burns
(chairman of the Fed Board of Governors) two days later.
[51] Ibid., p. 2.

pluses.[52] The report could not have been very comforting to those bankers who feared market disturbances.[53]

In sum, a wide spectrum of policy makers and market participants feared the effect of recycling on financial markets. Problems included loss of confidence in the interbank market after the collapse of Herstatt and Franklin National, skewed yield differentials between credit markets for various types of instruments, unbalanced maturity distribution of liabilities and assets, and swings in the money supply from shifting funds between banks with different reserve ratios. In addition, there was the vulnerability of financial markets to political blackmail by OPEC nations, the problem of U.S. debt crowding out domestic credit markets, and the simple perception that recycling would not be "automatic" and therefore leaving it to markets would threaten their stability. The solution to nearly all of these problems was for the government to recycle petrodollars and absolve markets of the responsibility.

RECONSTRUCTING LEGITIMACY

Calming Markets

There can be little doubt that bankers and policy makers were worried that recycling would overburden the ability of capital markets. David Rockefeller won literary renown for his observation: "What we see ahead are treacherous economic seas and gale-force financial winds, strong enough to capsize even large and well-manned ships—unless sails are reefed early, and all hands are ready at their stations when the gale hits."[54] Rockefeller's concern focused on the practice of lending by private banks to LDC governments. Banks would quickly reach "the limits of prudent credit exposure," and OPEC countries would be unlikely to continue to deposit revenues in the banking system. Furthermore,

[52] A central banker who visited the Saudi Arabian Monetary Agency (SAMA) in 1974 recalled seeing only one telex machine with which to place billions of dollars. In early 1975 an investment banker newly hired to advise SAMA found two telexes and billions of dollars in short call deposits (deposits that can be withdrawn on short notice). Interviews with Richard Debs (former vice-president in the Federal Reserve Bank of New York), New York, 14 September 1983, and David Mulford (formerly of White Weld), Princeton, New Jersey, 1983.

[53] Logue, "Petro Dollars and Chaos in U.S. Financial Markets." Another report on the threat of a sudden shift by OPEC was Adams and Fleisig, "Reduction of Short-Term Capital Inflows from OPEC to the United States."

[54] Actually, Rockefeller made this colorful statement in 1980, but it reflected his earlier opinions, which were stated with only double or triple metaphors. See Rockefeller, "Rough Seas Ahead."

"this form of recycling is not even a temporary solution for lesser-developed countries . . . which are not in a position to borrow at all." To solve the problems, Rockefeller called for "a new era of international cooperation."[55]

As they are clearly aware, public statements by leaders in the financial services industry affect market confidence. By 1976, having increased their exposure to LDCs, bankers made public statements attesting to the strength of capital markets and the ability of those markets to recycle efficiently and automatically without government intervention.

Of this genre of statement, the best known is Citibank chairman Walter Wriston's argument that "countries cannot go bankrupt."[56] Whether Wriston really believed in the soundness of lending to LDCs or he simply wanted to boost public confidence in his bank cannot be known. The head of a prominent British merchant bank, Lord Lever, called Wriston "the fairy of world banking for his obsessive optimism."[57] And as Darrell Delamaide points out, "Countries may not go bankrupt, but over the years many investors have gone bankrupt because of loans to such countries."[58]

When policy makers and bankers fear the stability of markets, they rarely make that fear public. Imagine what the head of a savings and loan would do when faced with a run on the bank by scared depositors. Rather than admitting to the shaky finances of her institution, she would probably make soothing statements to bolster the depositors' confidence. Statements by government officials and bankers on the efficacy of markets to recycle petrodollars were attempts to convince the public to retain confidence in financial markets. These statements tell us more about the agreed ways that things should have worked than the way they actually did work.

In public, bankers put on a brave face and testified to the ability of market forces to solve the world's problems. In private, they voiced their fears to government officials, who responded by issuing research reports assuring banks that international markets were sound. Telling a banker that markets are sound would appear to be preaching to the converted. Yet in retrospect, the public declarations of bankers and economic policy makers predicting that recycling would occur automati-

[55] David Rockefeller, "Financial Aspects of the Energy Situation."

[56] Ironically, this point was first made by Thomas W. Lamont, a partner at J. P. Morgan & Co. in the 1920s, while he was rescheduling Mexican debt. See Bodayla, "Bankers versus Diplomats."

[57] Quoted in Delamaide, *Debt Shock*, p. 31.

[58] Ibid., p. 98.

cally were little more than the theatrical statements of scared men who hoped that if they repeated that nothing was wrong often enough there was a chance things would actually turn out all right. Our conventional wisdom on the automaticity of markets for petrodollar recycling was motivated by the instrumental rationality of policy makers and bankers. It was their attempt to calm markets and not an unbiased observation of empirical evidence.

The Legitimacy of Market Forces

In a speech to the joint meeting of the directors of the IMF and the World Bank in 1974, William Simon expressed satisfaction with early processes of recycling petrodollars:

> So far, our existing complex of financial mechanisms, private and intergov-
> ernmental, has proved adequate to the task of recycling the large volumes
> of oil monies already moving in the system. Initially the private financial
> markets played the major role, adapting in imaginative and constructive
> ways. More recently, government-to-government channels have increas-
> ingly been opened, and they will play a more important role as time goes
> by.

He solemnly vowed that the "U.S. Government offers no special subsidies or inducements to attract capital here," although that was exactly what he, as a representative of the government, was doing.[59]

Simon's words contradicted his acts. The acts were done in secret, while the words were offered to the two institutions that constitute the international monetary regime. This, then, is a striking example of a public justification that reveals the legitimate norms by which the U.S. government justified its policies to the IMF. "Financial mechanisms, private and intergovernmental," were the legitimate institutions through which recycling was to be channeled. If possible, adjustment would be left to market forces. To the extent that markets could not adapt, the guiding hand of intergovernmental coordination should consign oil monies to nations with oil-related trade deficits. Interactions between central monetary institutions was desired, but unilateral action to attract Arab capital was against the implicit rules.

[59] Statement of Treasury Secretary Simon before the Boards of Governors of the International Monetary Fund and the International Bank for Reconstruction and Development, Washington, D.C., 1 October 1974; reprinted in Department of State *Bulletin* 71, no. 1844, 28 October 1974; p. 576.

Simon laboriously objected to calling recruitment of Saudi capital bilateralism. In testimony to Congress he differentiated between what he had done and what would be a bilateral deal: "To go and make unconstrained bilateral deals involving oil at exorbitant prices, was what we [Simon and Kissinger] were strongly opposed to."[60] Matters of finance were by their very nature bilateral, Simon argued, and therefore there was nothing uncooperative about discussions between the U.S. and Saudi governments on where the latter should invest its funds.

This statement, however, is clearly more of an appeal to legitimate norms than a successful application of them. Buying oil from a foreign nation is also by its nature bilateral, but the objectionable action comes in bidding the price up. Similarly, with financial instruments, the United States did nothing wrong by discussing investment with the Saudis. Providing market incentives for the Saudis to buy T-bills was, however, outside of the bounds of legitimate action as defined by Simon.

A considerable drawback to the influx of Saudi capital into the United States, however it was gained, was the definition of legitimate accountability proscribed in at least one congressional study. According to the House Committee on Banking and Currency, the advantages of Arab investment in Treasury securities also carried a responsibility to allocate funds for foreign balance-of-payments adjustment: "The Government must recognize that the more OPEC money it can attract in its own coffers, the greater its responsibility to insure adequate recycling to countries with legitimate balance-of-payments financing requirements."[61] The "responsibility" of the U.S. government in international affairs is obviously in the realm of how legitimate authority is perceived. Yet by the same token, "responsibility to insure adequate recycling" can also be seen as the power to allocate resources. While the U.S. government had a legitimate responsibility to recycle the petrodollars it managed to attract, it also had the power to make other nations come to terms for access to those funds.

The definitions of the situation and legitimate policy responses to it were heavily characterized by embedded liberalism. International adjustment was to be effected by open capital markets and free trade, but the United States would reserve the "right" to protect the domestic economy from the unwanted consequences of a liberal international economic order. Individual nations were not to compete to bring their trade accounts into balance, according to Shultz, because that would

[60] U.S. Congress, Senate, Committee on Finance, *Economic Implications*, p. 19.
[61] U.S. Congress, House, Committee on Banking and Currency, *Petrodollars*, p. 8.

mean a round of competitive beggar-thy-neighbor policies. Similarly, nations needed to cooperate to offer investment incentives to OPEC members so that they would produce more oil than would otherwise be in their economic interests. In other words, market forces were to allocate resources among industrialized nations, but those market forces were to be shaped by economic incentives and collective action by the leading economies.

Given this contradictory definition of legitimacy, by which market forces were to allocate value but the market forces themselves were to be shaped by political action, it is not surprising that Treasury officials faced a difficult task in defining the bounds of legitimate market intervention. Officials of the Treasury Department saw bilateral negotiations with OPEC as illegitimate except insofar as they were characterized by market forces but not the laws of supply and demand. Simon's definition of bilateralism, for instance, was when nations bid up the price of oil. If they bought oil but did not change the price to other producers, it was a legitimate economic transaction. Market forces were to predomine, except when those market forces were disadvantageous to the industrialized world.

By this definition of legitimacy, the United States was permitted to garner the lion's share of Arab capital but only if American policy makers did not actively seek it. Dealing with the Saudis on a central bank to central bank basis was desirable, as was offering the Saudis an incentive to produce more oil by *collectively* putting together an investment fund. Unilaterally offering the Saudis an incentive to invest in U.S. government obligations was not considered cooperative. If the money ended up in U.S. capital markets by virtue of market forces, the United States had the responsibility to recycle those funds to nations with an oil-related trade deficit. It was, however, not legitimate for the United States to make other nations come to terms for those funds. Using U.S. power to construct market forces resembling the status quo ante was fine. Using power to take advantage of the new status quo was not.

Officials of the State Department, Treasury, and Federal Reserve System saw the problem of recycling as a single play Prisoners' Dilemma. If nations acted unilaterally to adjust their trade deficits or to attract OPEC capital, a global welfare loss comparable to the Great Depression would ensue. Therefore, nations had to cooperate. Recycling required cooperation, but it was also defined as facilitating cooperation in the issue areas of trade and access to oil. If nations were not strapped for balance-of-payments financing, they would not be so tempted to initiate beggar-thy-neighbor policies. If an attractive investment fund could be

44

established for OPEC, it would have an incentive to produce more oil, and nations would not be so tempted to bid up the price unilaterally.

Policy makers defined the legitimate response to the oil shock as avoiding unilateral autarkic policies. They expressed an implicit assumption that international economic adjustment should be accomplished through unbridled market forces. So long as petrodollar recycling did not threaten the stability of international capital markets, and the international balance of payments was not too disequilibrated, legitimate financial adjustment would occur through markets and not state action. Yet if the stability of markets was threatened, the United States reserved the right to protect the domestic economy from the unwanted consequences of a liberal international economic order.

To break into the loop of structure and agency (so as not to make a tautology of structure and agency), I focused on political leadership in the United States using a methodology suggested by Robert C. Tucker. This method entails examining a situation from the perspective of how leaders recognize and define it. To prevent imposing my own intellectual constructs on the recycling of petrodollars, I presented the perceptions of policy makers (where possible, in their own words).

I have also endeavored to establish a baseline for the idea of international legitimacy so that the following chapters can measure the extent to which U.S. hegemony has deviated from its own definitions of legitimate leadership. To examine this tricky issue of legitimacy, I presented the public statements of policy makers, both when they attempted to define legitimate actions and when they were defending their own actions. In defining how states should react to the oil shock and in defending their own actions, the policy makers attempted to persuade their audience by resorting to shared language and shared norms. These norms did not necessarily have anything to do with why or how policy makers acted, but in the process of justifying their actions the policy makers revealed their own conceptions of legitimate rule.

The problem of recycling petrodollars prompted four areas of concern. First was the instability of the interbank capital markets, which was caused by two large bank failures and deeply exacerbated by shifts of deposits from oil buyers to OPEC nations. A second area of concern was how to control wild fluctuations in banks' deposit bases and loan-reserve ratios caused by these shifts in deposits. This problem was one of control. Fed officials could not ensure stability if they could not "see" where the petrodollars were coming from, and to do this they wanted the petrodollars to be in the United States and under their control. A third concern was that harmful fluctuations in capital markets might occur if OPEC nations were to institute pernicious policies of massive deposit shifts. This concern reflected a new source of vulnerability in the United States to swings in the international political economy.

A final and very important concern was that automaticity of international balance-of-payments adjustment was unlikely. Makers of foreign economic policy saw no inherent reason why the surplus of oil-exporting states should eventually find its way to nations with an oil-related trade deficit. Not only were markets unable to handle the funds, but the Fed was unable to stabilize the markets, and the nation was unable to protect itself against pernicious foreign financial policies; but even if everything went smoothly in financial markets, there was no logical reason for the markets to act as a recycling mechanism.

Although the perceptions and definitions by policy makers are presented in this book along bureaucratic divisions, there is very little to suggest that where one sat determined where one stood. Each executive agency had certain responsibilities and defined the situation accordingly. The Fed worried more about the stability of international markets than did the Department of State, and the Treasury was more concerned than any other agency about how to fund the federal budget deficit. Yet none of these definitions of the situation were appreciably different, and none led to bureaucratic quarrels. Indeed, the policy implications of each bureaucracy, and their understanding of the legitimate role of markets, were fairly synonymous.

The Treasury and Fed had very specific concerns related to their bureaucratic areas of responsibility. Their worry was that the U.S. economy would slide into a recession if the government could not borrow foreign capital to fund the budget deficit. This concern was symptomatic of the systemic constraints facing a declining hegemon. As domestic expectations continued to rise while the willingness to pay for them fell, the government was unwilling to raise taxes. Instead, it saw surplus OPEC capital as a new opportunity to delay domestic adjustment.

It appeared that convincing the American public to spend less and save more had approximately the same chance as a snowball in Riyadh. The alternative, Arab investment, was a clear policy choice. Given a choice of adhering to the international legitimate precepts of multilateralism or meeting its responsibility to collect funds for government spending, Treasury officials chose to recruit Arab capital unilaterally.

Top officials of the Department of State saw the problem of recycling as a single-play Prisoners' Dilemma. They realized that nations would have an incentive to defect and predicted a return of the Great Depression if they did not cooperate. At most, State Department officials defined the situation as a crisis that might cause a loss in global welfare if nations acted unilaterally. At the very least, they circumscribed a notion of international legitimacy in which unilateral autarkic policies were illegitimate.

Although it is difficult to find much evidence that economic policy makers think in terms of grand strategy and broad political overtones, one statement by the chairman of the Federal Reserve Bank Board of Governors attests to his deep concern over the direction of the international political economy. Burns told the Joint Economic Committee of Congress:

> Financial cooperation is important; it can contribute to international economic and political stability in the face of large oil deficits. But financial cooperation alone is not enough. Even with an orderly financing of deficits, the immense burden of carrying and ultimately repaying the debts will still remain. Financial cooperation may ease the transition, but it does not answer the most troublesome question: "A transition to *what?*"[62]

In general, the United States and industrialized nations as a whole sought to reestablish a previous equilibrium of market forces that produced outcomes to their benefit. Initially, the rise in the price of oil was seen as temporary, and governments in the industrialized world saw the problem as one of restoring the price to its past level. That period passed quickly, but perceptions in the mid-1970s were consistent. To the extent that adjustment was accepted as necessary by the U.S. government, the need for adjustment was defined as the need for retaining America's place in the international hierarchy of power and wealth.

In the absence of a global agreement to distribute all petrodollars through international political institutions, the only policy that would satisfy all of the early perceptions of recycling was to recruit Saudi funds into government obligations in an account physically held by the Fed. All of the actors agreed (more or less) to the danger of competitive beggar-thy-neighbor policies by nations attempting unilaterally to bring their trade accounts into balance. Most agreed on the danger of abrupt shifts in Arab funds. The Treasury seemed reassured that such shifts would not cause problems but feared that U.S. government borrowing

---

[62] Federal Reserve *Bulletin*, December 1974, pp. 832–34.

in private capital markets was about to disrupt the economy. There was no agency in the U.S. government (aside from anti-Arab congressmen—which came later) that had any reason to oppose recruitment of Arab funds, and many actively supported it. It should not be a great surprise, then, to find that recruiting Arab funds into T-bills is exactly what the U.S. government did.

CHAPTER THREE

Making Markets Work

If we are to understand petrodollar recycling, we need a picture of capital flows and where they went. This is particularly important given the pervasive thesis that markets were responsible for recycling petrodollars. If markets alone were responsible, recycling would make a poor case study for heuristic observations about how value is allocated in the international political economy. Thus in this chapter I evaluate the view that market forces recycled petrodollars and present a picture of capital flows after the oil shock. This task is not as simple as it might seem. The meaning of the phrase *market forces worked* is subject to many varying interpretations and means of evaluation. How one goes about testing market forces is a difficult problem. The three objectives of this chapter are to understand the view in the literature that markets recycled petrodollars, to evaluate that view, and to present a picture of petrodollar recycling that is drawn inductively from the data rather than being deduced from theories of international economics.

What it means for markets to work, and what that meant for the specific case of recycling, are the problems that motivate this chapter. The following section explores how to define and measure market forces. The following two sections derive testable propositions from the literature and then test them. A final section presents a new picture of recycling. The goal is to answer two basic questions: Was recycling achieved by credit markets? And if not, what were the mechanics of getting capital surpluses to finance capital deficits?

The Conventional Wisdom

What Are Markets?

When the price of crude oil fell in the mid-1980s, more than one decade after petrodollar recycling began, the chief economist of a Wall Street economic advisory firm wrote in the *New York Times*:

> American banks have loaned more than $100 billion to the developing countries, a carry-over from the days when they were merrily "recycling petrodollars" from the OPEC countries. Loans to Mexico alone amount to more than $25 billion.
>
> [Danger of default comes from] severe financial problems already evident in Mexico, Venezuela, Nigeria and other oil-exporting countries.[1]

If Third World debt was created by recycling petrodollars from OPEC countries, then why is it that many of the countries now holding most of the credit and in danger of default are oil exporters? Common sense should tell us that this view of recycling bears further examination.

The view often repeated in the literature is that recycling was achieved by private credit markets. The challenge to the international monetary system was made moot by floating exchange rates, and the hidden hand of market forces resolved the disequilibrium in the global balance of payments. When we sit down to analyze this thesis, however, it is not clear what it means for markets to work, or what it means for petrodollar recycling to have been effected by markets.

The view most commonly expressed in the literature is that banks, acting as intermediaries, lent OPEC capital to oil-importing LDCs. It makes little sense from the standpoint of economic theory to expect that private credit markets would lend money to LDCs hit hardest by the oil shock. Instead, we would expect that banks lent funds to nations that did not face higher oil bills. Nations without access to credit markets were, therefore, forced to adjust by importing less oil (or they had to turn to official creditors). But if that is the case, and market forces worked despite the fact that there was no relation between oil imports and new credit, then what would the world have looked like in the absence of market forces or if market forces had not worked?

There are very few instances of pure markets. In any case where markets play a role in balance-of-payments adjustment financing, governments are dominant actors. When a government is a buyer or seller in a

---

[1] Sam Nakagama, "Fallout from the Oil Plunge," *The New York Times*, 16 February 1986, p. F3.

market for securities, analysts nonetheless maintain that the market is producing outcomes. Even when the government is—for a time—the only seller of a commodity (e.g., Treasury bills) economists say that the yields on T-bills are brought about by the price mechanism. Yet it is clear that in some instances governments and institutions bring about outcomes outside of markets. If the IMF allows a member to draw down its quota, this is not called market forces. What differentiates between market forces and balance-of-payments adjustment financing from the IMF? When governments deposit their capital in a private bank, and then borrow money from a private bank, is that any more a form of market forces than the IMF?

The very idea of international markets is internally contradictory. *International* by its etymology tells us that the world is divided into nation-states. Nation-states open their borders to international commerce by choice, and in the realm of international finance the only commodity that they produce (specie money) is traded and bartered across state frontiers. *International capital markets* thus refers to an ideal type of a world with no governments and no national borders but also is driven by the study of an issue area that exists by virtue of the nation-state system. To the extent that the pure ideal type of international markets exists, it is a world without nations that is defined by a world of nations.

Finding Testable Propositions

The description of petrodollar recycling most prevalent in the literature attributes allocation of balance-of-payments financing to private markets. OPEC had a structural trade surplus from 1974 to 1981, and less developed countries bore the corresponding deficit. To fund that deficit LDCs borrowed money from private international lenders (i.e., banks or buyers of bonds), and the capital they borrowed was supplied in the first place by the deposits of OPEC governments.

In these descriptions, particularly the earliest ones, there is an element of surprise that private markets worked to recycle petrodollars because neither economists nor policy makers expected markets to behave so nicely. Governments of LDCs did not previously have much access to bank credit because they were deemed uncreditworthy. It was supposed to be the job of the IMF to resolve balance-of-payments imbalances, assisted by bilateral government-to-government loans. Now, thought economists, the hidden hand of market forces would solve balance-of-payments adjustment problems automatically and efficiently.

Robert Z. Aliber, author of a popular text on the international monetary system, wrote that at first "the financial collapse of the West seemed imminent" because it was feared that the money would somehow disappear from the system. But Aliber explains that the OPEC nations could not bury the money, and "money paid for oil imports is recycled automatically."[2]

Brian Tew agreed that "financing is automatic" because OPEC members had to put their money in banks, and banks had to lend that money to someone else.[3] *The Politics of International Economic Relations*, by Joan Spero, is the textbook that is most widely read in university courses on international political economy. She noted that OPEC's surplus dollars "were recycled primarily through private banks which lent these funds to oil-importing countries."[4]

This view gained currency in the economics literature after it was voiced by public officials. The vice-president of the New York Fed, for example, expressed relief over "the ability of the private banking system to handle the petro-dollar flows."[5] George Shultz, then the Treasury Secretary, commented:

> Far from collapsing under the weight of the petrodollar problem, financial markets thus worked to solve that problem. . . .
>
> While governments were meeting to work out the details of the Safety Net [a multilateral recycling scheme that was never realized, see Chapter Four], world financial markets were quietly doing much recycling on their own. Countries with large deficits borrowed in the Eurodollar market and from large commercial banks in the industrialized countries with the strongest currencies.[6]

To be sure, there were differing views. Benjamin J. Cohen pointed out in two different books that oil exporters were among the biggest borrowers from private banks and that the hardest-hit oil importers had the most difficult time borrowing from private banks. In 1981 he described a mismatch in international markets between oil-surplus depos-

[2] Aliber, *International Money Game*, 5th ed., pp. 137, 140, and 141.

[3] Tew, *Evolution of the International Monetary System*, p. 190.

[4] Spero, *Politics of International Economic Relations*, 4th ed. p. 47. She is quick to point out that recycling also took place through international organizations and through government treasuries, but she concludes that "the private system, especially the banking system, was the primary monetary manager."

[5] Debs, "Address," p. 127.

[6] Shultz and Dam, *Economic Policy Beyond the Headlines*, pp. 192 and 193. Further examples of the conventional wisdom in official sources include Solomon, "The Allocation of Oil Deficits," and IMF *World Outlook*, June 1981.

itors and oil-deficit borrowers.[7] Yet even he, in 1986, wrote that for petrodollar recycling, "funds flowed from oil exporters through the intermediation of international banks to oil-importing countries and back again."[8] Jeffry Frieden points out that the first oil shock "increased the need of such oil importers as Brazil to borrow and improved the creditworthiness of such oil exporters as Venezuela and Mexico." Still, he describes the effect of the oil shocks as creating "major payments deficits for the oil-importing LDCs that borrowing helped cover."[9]

In short, the view that in the 1970s OPEC put a lot of money in banks, banks lent a lot of money to LDCs, and LDCs then spent that money on oil is dominant and pervasive. To avoid the accusation that I am setting up a straw man with my description of the conventional wisdom, I conducted a random sample of all HG3881 entries (the Library of Congress designation for books on the international monetary system) in the catalog computer at the central library of Rutgers, the State University of New Jersey. The list contained over 250 entries written before 1985 (books written since then are not as likely to mention recycling), and the sample consists of ten books chosen with a random number generator. Three books did not mention recycling at all and seven books share the liberal economic thesis of recycling. An example from 1983:

> From 1973 onwards, world events put these [the Eurobank] markets to the fore following the quadrupling of oil prices as they became the ideal vehicle through which the OPEC "petro-dollar" surpluses could be channeled, and from which the consuming nations—both the advanced and, increasingly, the non-oil less developed countries could shore up their balance of payments deficits, as the oil and Arab nations were unwilling and then unable to assume the credit risks implied by such recycling operations.[10]

A random sample of books written between 1985 and 1995 produced similar results, although explanations of why the market worked were a bit more sophisticated, and recycling was less likely to be mentioned.[11]

---

[7] Cohen, *Banks and the Balance of Payments*.

[8] Cohen, *In Whose Interest*, p. 25.

[9] Frieden, *Debt, Development, and Democracy*, pp. 62–63.

[10] Johns, *Tax Havens and Offshore Finance*. The other books in the sample were Aliber, *International Money Game*, chap. 7; Carbaugh and Fan, *International Monetary System*, pp. 143–44; Davis, *Management Function in International Banking*, pp. 19 and 23; McKenzie, *Economics of the Euro-Currency System*, pp. 120ff; Oliver, *International Economic Co-operation and the World Bank*, pp. x–xi; and Versluysen, *Political Economy of International Finance*.

[11] The ten books in that sample were Aliber, *International Money Game*, 5th ed.; Aliber, ed., *Reconstruction of International Monetary Arrangements*; Capie, *Monetary Economics in the 1980s*; Corden, *Inflation, Exchange Rates and the World Economy*; Fraser and Long, *World Fi-*

Each of the authors has a somewhat different view of petrodollar recycling, but they may be summarized and grouped into three categories. The first view is that recycling was accomplished by market forces because the bulk of the OPEC capital surplus was placed in markets. By definition, whatever markets did was recycling, and also by definition, whatever markets did was "market forces." Hence recycling was accomplished by markets. This view is proven correct when we can demonstrate that OPEC nations did place the preponderance of their surpluses in capital markets and when those capital markets did not fail. It does not tell us much, however, about the role of markets in international political economy. The view tends toward tautology in that recycling is defined as whatever markets did. There is little possibility, given this definition of recycling, that it could have been brought about by anything but market forces.

A second view defines recycling as a process of intermediation between savers (OPEC) and borrowers. Intermediation does not necessarily have to be effected by private international banks—it is more than possible that an international financial organization, a multilateral development bank, or even a bilateral aid donor could serve as an intermediary. To say that recycling was brought about by markets is, therefore, a falsifiable statement. If an increased need for intermediation suddenly arose, and international capital markets fulfilled that function, then we should expect to see growth in the size of those markets commensurate with the size of the OPEC surplus. Indeed, there are many references in the literature to the exponential growth of the Eurobanking market following the oil shock, and banks are said to have been "flush with petrodollars."[12]

When banks lend money, they are serving as intermediaries between savers and borrowers. If banks create borrowers, then whatever they did was intermediation so long as OPEC deposited its capital with them. The proposition that recycling was brought about by intermediation does not tell us what the world would have looked like in its absence. It would be improper to test whether the OPEC surplus went to nations

---

nancial System; Kambata, *Practice of Multinational Banking*; Robert Morris Associates, *Guide to Analyzing Foreign Banks*; Swary, *Global Financial Deregulation*; Suzuki, *Evolution of the International Monetary System*; and Watson, *International Capital Markets.*

[12] For examples of this claim, see Cohen, *In Whose Interest*, p. 39; Makin, *Global Debt Crisis*, p. 29; and Spero, *Politics of International Economic Relations*, 3rd ed., p. 59. Lissakers argues against this view in *Banks, Borrowers, and the Establishment*, p. 23; and Frieden points out that OPEC states began depositing money in Euromarkets long before the oil shocks, in *Banking on the World*, pp. 82 and 85.

with oil-related deficits because there is no reason for financial intermediaries to allocate value based on need. We cannot evaluate the extent
to which banks distributed capital according to risk-adjusted rates of return because there is no way to measure rates of return or risk except to
impute it from outcomes. We know that much of the international lending engaged in by banks ran into trouble one decade later, but we do
not know what the alternatives might have been. Finally, we know which
nations demanded debt because of current account deficits, but we do
not know how those current account deficits came about. Nations that
had access to international credit enjoyed the prospect of being able to
run a current account deficit. Nations to which banks would not lend
money did not have that prospect—they had to adjust and import less.
It is possible that market forces allocated the distribution of current account deficits following the oil shock, and recycling is simply a description of anything that private actors did with OPEC capital. In short, we
do not know what the world would have looked like in the absence of
market forces, which makes it difficult to evaluate their efficacy in allocating value.

A third view is more difficult to discern in the literature, and it is the
only view that is truly possible to test. This description holds that recycling was the process whereby the money gained by means of an oil-related trade surplus went to fund deficits caused by more expensive oil
imports. It is still possible in this description for the distribution of current account deficits to be determined by the recycling process. It is,
however, less likely that recycling would be a cause rather than an effect
because the description refers to a specific commodity, not the entire
structure of imports. If we find that nations with increased oil import
bills used private credit to fund their current account deficits, and that
there was a correlation between having higher oil import bills and having access to credit, then this view of recycling would be confirmed.

TESTING PROPOSITIONS THAT MARKETS WORKED

Global Balance of Payments

Many analyses of recycling start with the presumption that OPEC had
all of the global trade surplus in the 1970s and the rest of the world
shared the corresponding deficit. In fact, the picture is a bit more complicated.

Figure 3.1 shows balances on goods and services for 1973 to 1981.
The figure splits advanced industrialized democracies into two groups:

55

FIGURE 3.1. Current account surpluses and deficits, 1973–1981.

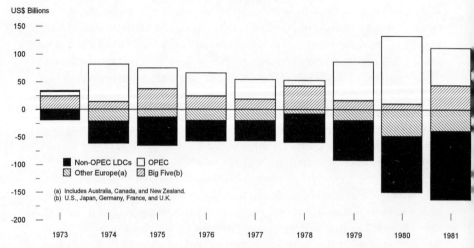

SOURCE: IMF, *International Financial Statistics, Supplement on Balance of Payments* (Washington, D.C., 1984). Dollar/SDR conversions based on period averages in IMF, *International Financial Statistics Year book* (Washington, D.C., 1984).

the five largest economies and "other industrialized."[13] In an average year (between 1973 and 1981), OPEC held two thirds of the surplus, and the remainder went to the major industrialized economies. Roughly one-third of the global trade deficit was held by "other industrialized" nations, and more than two thirds was accounted for by non-OPEC LDCs. Excluding Turkey and Greece, industrialized nations together had a net trade surplus throughout the period. The industrialized world as a whole ran a net surplus, and it was therefore an exporter of capital. The deficit by LDCs corresponded not only to OPEC's surplus but to the surplus of the developed economies as well.

Those industrialized economies with deficits (i.e., those not in the "Big Five") required foreign capital to cover their trade imbalance, but they also had easy access to European credit markets, in which they are active participants as holders of both assets and liabilities. Private credit markets in industrialized countries were net lenders to the rest of the world from 1973 to 1981. They lent more money to LDCs (both importers and exporters of oil) and East Bloc economies than they took in as deposits from those countries.[14] Borrowing by the other industrialized

[13] The "other industrialized" category includes the rest of Western Europe (and Turkey and Greece), as well as Australia, Canada, and New Zealand.

[14] See Dennis, *International Financial Flows*, esp. pp. 46–51. The figures can be derived

countries was not an example of recycling because the credit pool they drew upon was not dependent on OPEC deposits. The other industrialized countries were, in effect, borrowing from the large industrialized countries. The nations that required financing for trade deficits were in the nonindustrialized world.

Placement of the Surplus

Table 3.1 shows the disposition of the OPEC investable surplus, including some aid flows (including loans but not outright grants).[15] It shows that by 1981 three-quarters of the total OPEC surplus was invested in industrialized nations. One-quarter was in the United States, another 25 percent was in the rest of the industrialized world, and 30 percent was deposited in Eurobanks. Indeed, if we combine the figures for OPEC placements in Eurobanks (which includes foreign branches of U.S. banks), domestic branches of U.S. banks, and British banks, bank deposits constituted 38 percent of all OPEC investments.[16]

At first glance, it would appear that 40 percent of this portfolio went to private banks while 20 percent was recycled directly to LDCs. It is important to remark the second to last row in Table 3.1 ("Net movements"), however, to get the whole picture. That line of figures shows that (for 1977) one-third of all bank deposits were matched by OPEC borrowing. In other words, there were $68 billion in bank deposits, but those deposits are offset by $23 billion that OPEC countries borrowed from banks. Bank deposits, net of borrowing, are approximately the same proportion of foreign assets as purchases of government debt and also the same proportion as direct loans to LDCs. Bank deposits (net), government debt, and loans to LDCs are each close to 20 percent of the portfolio. The rest of the total is accounted for by market investments other than government debt (stocks, bonds, and direct investment),

---

from Bank for International Settlements, "Maturity Distribution of International Bank Lending."

[15] It must be emphasized that these figures, compiled by the Bank of England, serve only as rough estimates. Of the ten or so government agencies, private banks, and international organizations that attempt to track the disposition of OPEC foreign assets, estimates differ by as much as 10 percent (which would lead to total errors of up to $35 billion). The Bank of England figures are in the mid-range of estimates.

[16] Many of these funds were held by banks as trustee accounts, which means that they may have ended up as investments in T-bills or equities. Kuwait had at least $7 billion in the U.S. stock market that was held as a trustee account by Citibank (Dorfman, "Kuwait Oil Profits Buy $7 Billion of U.S. Securities"), and the Saudis are reported to have made T-bill investments through some of their trustee accounts.

TABLE 3.1. Net change in the deployment of OPEC's capital surplus, 1974–1982 ($ billions).

	1974	1975	1976	1977	1978	1979	1980	1981	1982	1982 level	1982 per-cent
United States											
Bank desposits	4.2	0.6	1.9	0.4	0.8	5.1	-1.2	-1.9	4.7	17.0	5
U.S. government obligations	6.2	4.2	6.3	3.8	-1.9	0.8	11.6	12.7	6.4	57.4	16
Other portfolio investment	1.1	3.2	3.0	3.1	1.6	1.1	4.7	4.6	-0.4	20.0	5
TOTAL	11.5	8.0	11.2	7.3	0.5	7.0	15.1	15.4	10.7	94.4	26
United Kingdom											
Sterling bank deposits	1.7	0.2	-1.6	0.3	0.1	1.5	1.4	0.5	1.2	5.0	1
British government stock	0.9	0.4	0.2	0.3	-0.4	0.2	2.1	0.9	0.1	3.2	1
Treasury bills	2.7	-0.9	-1.1	-0.3	0.1	—	-0.1	-0.1	—	0.1	0
Other sterling placements[a]	0.7	0.3	0.5	0.4	0.1	0.4	0.2	0.2	-0.6	2.0	1
TOTAL	6.0	0.0	-2.0	0.7	-0.1	2.1	3.6	1.5	0.7	10.3	3
Eurocurrency Deposits in U.K. and bank deposits in other industrialized countries[b]	23.9	9.3	12.5	12.5	3.0	34.8	43.9	2.7	-21.9	116.1	32
Other investments in other industrialized countries[a]	3.4	7.4	5.9	5.7	3.7	3.6	15.0	19.6	6.7	71.6	20
IMF and World Bank[a]	3.5	5.3	1.5	—	-0.4	-0.5	3.3	2.3	2.1	18.6	5
Loans to developing countries	4.9	6.5	6.4	7.0	6.2	9.7	6.3	7.2	3.9	54.0	15
Reductions (−) in deployed assets	53.2	36.5	35.5	33.2	12.9	55.7	87.2	48.7	2.2	365.0	100
Net movements[c]	n/a	3.0	9.0	11.0	11.0	2.0	4.0	8.4	19.8		
Current balance	n/a	31.8	36.0	24.7	-2.9	58.2	108.6	48.9	-13.9		

[a]Mainly loans and holdings of equities.
[b]Includes foreign branches of U.S. banks.
[c]Net borrowing by OPEC countries.
SOURCE: Bank of England.

OPEC lending to itself through the banking system, and loans to the IMF and World Bank.

What is important, then, is the data on where individual nations with capital surpluses invested their funds. Unfortunately, the data for individual OPEC nations are extremely difficult to get. The Bank for International Settlements (BIS) collects data by nationality on who owes what to whom in the Eurobanking market. For OPEC nations, however, the BIS would not give figures for individual countries from 1974 until 1984.[17] OPEC investments in the United States are classified as "top secret" for reasons that are discussed in Chapter 5 (this security classification seemed to change for Iranian investments in 1979 and for Iraqi investments in 1990).

Table 3.2 shows figures for Saudi Arabia and Kuwait.[18] The figures are for different years, which makes detailed comparison risky, and the percentages are rounded to the nearest 5 percent because (despite the great secrecy that surrounds them) there is probably a 5 to 10 percent margin of error. The only figure that is definitely accurate is that for Saudi purchases of U.S. government debt.

A full 30 percent of Saudi Arabia's portfolio was in an account of the New York Federal Reserve Bank, and that made up 70 percent of all Saudi assets in the United States. Almost all of the remainder was in banks, but a great deal of these deposits were offset by bank lending to

[17] The ostensible reason was to protect the privacy of individual institutions. In fact, the BIS practiced this principle only for OPEC. In 1984 the BIS began to release data on individual OPEC nations, but U.S. banks would not report to the BIS in such a way as to make such disclosure possible for them. As a result, the BIS figures do not include the foreign branches of U.S. banks, and that makes them fairly useless. For some of this period, no agency in the U.S. government kept figures on the foreign assets or liabilities of U.S. banks. For an excellent and informed account, see Lissakers, *Banks, Borrowers, and the Establishment*, chap. 2.

[18] I compiled these data by making rough estimates based on unpublished documents and public data sources. The former included "Saudi Exchange Rate Policy," a single page from a 1978 classified Treasury memo (with no identifying marks except for "Confidential, declassified, authority: Russell Munk, 9/10/79"), and page 3 of a CIA memo from the Office of International Banking and Portfolio Investment, drafted by David Curry, reviewed by F. L. Widman, 21 November 1978, and marked "classified by CIA:DB 312/01645-78, exempt from general declassification schedule of executive order 11652 exemption category 5 b(2)." I then showed the rough estimates to several government officials in a branch of the U.S. Treasury, which was responsible for collecting and aggregating OPEC data. One official corrected the estimate of Saudi purchases of U.S. government obligations as being far too low. Two other officials then confirmed the revised estimates as being correct. The figures were also confirmed by officials at the Saudi Arabian Monetary Agency, but they were less likely to know the Saudi investment position of the previous decade than the sources in the U.S. Treasury. Since these interviews were conducted (1983 to 1985), several newspaper articles have referred to Saudi investments in T-bills.

THE HIDDEN HAND OF AMERICAN HEGEMONY

TABLE 3.2. Estimated Saudi and Kuwaiti claims on foreigners (rounded to nearest 5% of foreign assets).

	Percent of Saudi portfolio[a]	Percent of Kuwaiti portfolio[b]
U.S. banks	5	5
Foreign branches of U.S. banks	15 ⎫	
Non-U.S. banks	25 ⎭	15
U.S. government	30	5
Direct investment in United States	—	5
Other Investment in United States	5	15
Total in United States	40	30
Total in U.S. dollars	80	50

[a]For end-1976. Since that time the total in U.S. dollars has decreased.
[b]For end-1982. Kuwaiti direct investment in the United States was not large in 1976.

other OPEC countries. Indeed, by the 1980s Saudi Arabia itself was among the top ten nonindustrialized borrowers in the world. Kuwait, by comparison, has devoted more of its foreign holdings to long-term investments, less to dollar denominated assets, and much less to U.S. government obligations.

As I discuss in more detail in Chapter 5, the United States government did not try to influence the investment decisions of Kuwait, but it did try to influence the investment decisions of Saudi Arabia. If we view Kuwaiti investment as a diversified portfolio, the composition of which is determined by basic financial principles, the Saudi investment in U.S. government obligations stands in stark contrast. Furthermore, since Saudi investment dwarfed capital flows by other OPEC nations, it is not only the Saudi portfolio but rather the OPEC portfolio in aggregate that was invested according to political criteria.

A significant part of OPEC's surplus was lent directly to Western governments. As I argue in Chapter 5, this investment was a result of U.S. policy.

Change in Euromarket Activities

If recycling involved intermediation by the international capital market between surplus and deficit countries, then we should observe both a change in the size of the market and a change in its lending behavior. If OPEC funds in T-bills displaced money into the Eurobanking market, then we should see extraordinary growth in the size of that market. Yet as we see in Figure 3.2, growth in the Eurocurrency market (net of inter-bank transfers) was exponential from 1969 to 1980, but there was

FIGURE 3.2. Net size of the Eurocurrency market, 1969–1980.

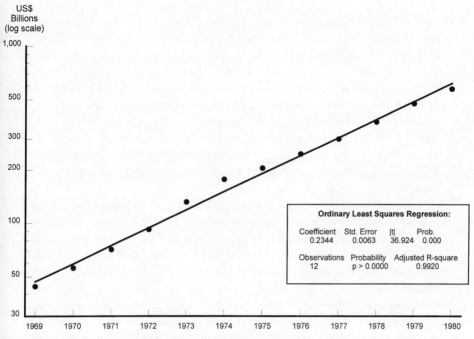

SOURCE: Bank for International Settlements, *Annual Reports*, various years.

not much extraordinary growth after the oil shock.[19] In fact, the exponential growth curve of the Eurocurrency market is so predictable that an ordinary least squares regression fitting a line to the data points is significant to p < 0.00001, and it accounts for 99.7 percent of the variance.

Despite the high level of confidence at which the regression is significant, an analysis of the residuals shows that the fitted line is slightly heteroscedastic.[20] This means that the Eurocurrency market was slightly larger from 1973 to 1976 than might be predicted, but it hardly leads to the conclusion that the market was flooded with petrodollars. When a

[19] A great majority of lending in the Eurocurrency market is simply the shifting of funds back and forth between Eurobanks, so the figures are for net size, which measures the borrowing and lending of the market as a whole to and from non-Eurobank institutions (individuals and firms).

[20] The residual is the amount by which a point differs from the prediction of the fitted line. Heteroscedasticity means that the values of the residuals show a persistent error in the predictions of the fitted line. In this case, the actual net size of the Eurodollar market was less than the prediction for all years except 1973 to 1976, when the data points were above the line.

line is fitted to all of the points *except* for 1973 to 1976, and then the deviation of the points for 1973 to 1976 is compared to the new baseline, the residual is most pronounced for 1974. In that year, the net size of the Eurocurrency market exceeded the predicted baseline by more than $35 billion, which was about 20 percent of the predicted net size. One must note, however, first, that the residuals begin in 1973, whereas OPEC deposits did not begin to accumulate until 1974. The surge in Eurocredit growth does correspond to the termination of the Bretton Woods agreement (widespread floating did not begin until 1973), and the myriad of regulations that were meant to insulate the American economy form the Eurocurrency market, including the Interest Equalization Tax, the Voluntary Foreign Credit Restraint program, and Regulation Q.[21]

A second observation from these data is that the market continued its exponential growth apparently unaffected by the small surge from 1973 to 1976. In short, it is difficult to associate growth in the Eurocurrency market with petrodollar deposits. According to the chief economists at three top Euromarket banks, the growth of the Euromarket depended almost wholly on U.S. monetary policy.[22] Many academic economists have expressed the same view.[23] The persistent claim that Eurobanks were bloated with petrodollars is not only inconsistent with the facts but inconsistent with recent economic literature as well.

Though the size of the Eurocurrency market and the ownership of its deposits does not seem to have changed appreciably after the oil shock, markets may have changed their lending behavior so as to intermediate between savers and deficit nations that had to borrow. A "balanced markets" approach in economic theory tells us that, all things being equal, a change in one market will produce an equilibrating change in all other related markets.[24] If Saudi Arabia chooses to invest call deposits at

---

[21] For more on these regulations, see Gowa, *Closing the Gold Window,* and for the effect of the regulations on Eurocurrency growth, see Johnston, *Economics of the Euro-Market.*

[22] Interviews with David Lomax, chief economist, National Westminister Bank; Geoffrey Maynard, chief economic adviser, Chase Manhattan Bank; and John Atkin, acting chief economist, Citibank; all in London, November and December 1984.

[23] After 1988, however, the correlation ends. In the absence of a good explanation to explain the current changes in the size of the Eurocurrency market, the sudden inefficacy of the model casts doubt on its explanatory power for the period before 1988. Interview with Christine M. Cummings, assistant vice-president for international capital markets, Federal Reserve Bank of New York, spring 1990.

[24] For examples, see Branson, Halthunen, and Masson, "Exchange Rates in the Short Run"; Dornbusch, "Portfolio Balance Model of the Open Economy"; and Tobin, "General Equilibrium Approach."

LIBOR, other Eurodollar deposits will be displaced and will end up in other markets.[25]

Many scholars have written that with the end of the Bretton Woods agreement, international capital markets inherited from the IMF the role of providing balance-of-payments adjustment financing.[26] The question, then, is whether there was a change in the source of balance-of-payments financing during the 1970s and whether the lending activity of the Eurocurrency market was related to increased oil deficits.

Indebtedness of the LDCs increased sharply during the 1970s and 1980s. The percentage of private credit that accounts for this indebtedness, however, did not changed noticeably. In 1970 private creditors accounted for 40 percent of all the disbursed outstanding debt guaranteed by LDC governments. That figure rose to 55 percent in 1975 and stood at 54 percent in 1980. It reached a peak in 1985 (58 percent) and fell to 47 percent in 1990. The increase from 40 to 54 percent in one decade is significant, but it cannot be taken to mean a wholesale shift from official sources to private markets. LDC indebtedness has increased at an exponential rate since 1970 (from $50 billion to nearly $1 trillion in 1990), but more than half of that debt is owed to official creditors. As Figure 3.3 depicts, debt from private lenders to LDC governments grew at a much faster rate during the 1970s than debt from official sources and private debt to private borrowers. All of the debt was growing at an exponential rate, however, and by 1980 the growth rate of publicly guaranteed debt from private lenders had leveled off to growth rates of other funding sources.

Another way to look at the question of whether private capital markets took over responsibility for balance-of-payments adjustment financing in the 1970s is to determine who received the credit. The IMF, after all, provided balance-of-payments adjustment financing to 150 members. If in the 1970s banks began to lend a significant proportion of their funds to just one country, and that country's government happened to guarantee the debt and use it for balance-of-payments adjustment, that does not indicate that banks began to lend money for balance-of-payments adjustment in general. All it tells us is that banks began to lend money to one country. What is significant is that the one country received so much financing, and to impute the generalization

---

[25] LIBOR is the London interbank offered rate, or the interest rate on deposits in the Eurobanking market.

[26] See Cohen, *Banks and the Balance of Payments*.

FIGURE 3.3. Sources of LDC finance, 1970–1981.

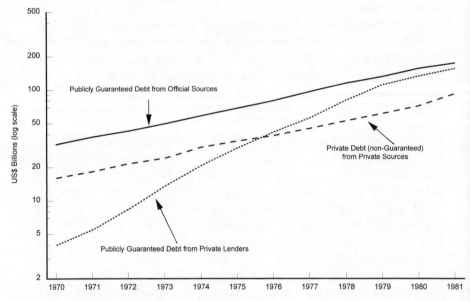

SOURCE: IBRD, *World Debt Tables* Data Disk, 1990.

that a movement toward balance-of-payments financing motivated lending to that one country would be false.

In 1970 just seventeen nations accounted for 51 percent of guaranteed private credit to all LDCs.[27] In 1975 the figure was the same, and in 1980 it rose marginally to 53 percent. World Bank statistics cover 130 LDCs, yet 17 received more than half of the private credit that was publicly guaranteed. This proportion did not change very much during the 1970s; nor indeed has it changed at any time since Eurocurrency markets began to operate. Although lending to all LDCs rose dramatically from 1960 to 1990, the proportion of publicly guaranteed debt that went to a small subset of nations remained the same. Even with involuntary lending for debt rescheduling, the figure did not rise above 60 percent in 1990.

By 1980, 29 percent of all publicly guaranteed lending to LDCs by private creditors went to oil-exporting nations. In 1970, those nations accounted for only 20 percent of publicly guaranteed lending to LDCs

[27] The World Bank lists seventeen highly indebted LDCs: Argentina, Bolivia, Brazil, Chile, Colombia, Costa Rica, the Ivory Coast, Ecuador, Jamaica, Mexico, Morocco, Nigeria, Peru, Philippines, Uruguay, Venezuela, and Yugoslavia.

by private creditors.[28] After the price of oil increased, those LDC governments with reserves borrowed 50 percent more of the credit pool than they had before. To the extent that there was intermediation, it may have been between oil exporters with savings and oil exporters who demanded credit.

By positing that recycling from oil-surplus states to oil-deficit states took place through credit markets, the prevalent view predicts a positive relationship between the increased amount of money that a country needs to pay for oil and the increased amount of credit it is able to secure from banks. This hypothesis can be tested by comparing new borrowing (guaranteed by governments) from 1973 to 1981 with increased oil expenses for the same period for each LDC. If the hypothesis is correct, we should see a positive relationship. The more a country was hit by big oil bills, the more it would have borrowed. If the proportion of credit lent to LDC governments was constant for a few oil-importing LDCs, but the growth in credit to those LDCs was caused by factors unrelated to the oil shock, then we should not expect to see a relationship between new borrowing and increased oil imports.

To analyze the relationship properly, we must divide each change (in oil imports and in new credit) by Gross National Product (GNP). Were we to compare the number of sheep and foreign trade in Vanuatu and the United States, we would surely find a strong correlation between the two. Do not, however, abandon your textbooks on trade theory (for this reason, at any rate). Sheep do not cause foreign trade. A large economy leads to both a greater number of farm animals and increased external commerce. To say something meaningful about sheep and trade, we would need to divide both figures to control for the sizes of the respective countries.

When the size of each economy is controlled for by dividing the data by GNP, there is no significant correlation between debt and oil deficits. If markets worked to intermediate between savers and nations with oil deficits, then we would expect to find a positive relationship between increased oil imports (as a proportion of GNP) and increased publicly guaranteed debt (as a proportion of GNP). In fact, there is no discernible relationship between the two variables.

An additional possibility is that recycling occurred in two stages, since there were two oil shocks. The first was in the end of 1973 and begin-

---

[28] IBRD, *World Debt Tables*, vol. 1. These percentages are for disbursed debt outstanding. The World Bank lists thirteen LDCs as oil exporters in debt. Some nations, such as Egypt and Syria, are included, and because oil is not a major export for them, they did require balance-of-payments adjustment financing.

ning of 1974, and the second was in 1979. Many economists differentiate between the processes of recycling after the first and the second oil shocks.[29] Therefore, to test the relationship between debt flows and oil payments properly, we too should differentiate between the two periods. Analyses of the data for 1973 to 1978 and for 1978 to 1981, however, do not yield significant results (Figure 3.4). For 1978 to 1981 the curve is an inverted U shape, suggesting the complete obverse of the prevalent view of recycling. The confidence level is 0.09—more than acceptable—but the adjusted R-square is less than 5 percent, meaning that the fitted line does not predict much of the data. Before these results are abandoned, however, one argument must be made in their favor. When 25 percent of the data points, randomly selected, are deleted from the sample, the coefficients remain nearly the same (i.e., they differ by less than the standard error), and the confidence level remains the same. Unfortunately, the adjusted R-square also remains the same. Thus increased expenditures on oil imports do not go very far in explaining increased publicly guaranteed debt to LDCs, and since the coefficient of the quadratic term is small, the effect that increased oil imports had on increased debt is relatively small. Yet to the extent that there is a relationship between the two variables, we may be confident that it has an inverted U shape. The nations that did not increase greatly expenditures on oil imports from 1978 to 1981 were more likely to receive credit from private banks. Nations that faced much larger oil bills did not receive much credit. The more oil exporters increased revenues from 1978 to 1981, the less likely they were to borrow from banks; and the less they increased revenues the more likely they were to take publicly guaranteed credit.

That there was no apparent relationship between increased debt and increased oil payments (over GNP) for 1973–78 and a possible inverted U-shaped relationship for 1978–81 is doubly significant. It tells us that credit markets did not intermediate between oil-export-derived savers and oil-importing borrowers during either period (following either oil shock), and for the second period the opposite may have happened. Intermediation took place between savers of all sorts and borrowers who did not have oil-related balance-of-payments adjustment financing needs.

It is also important that the significance of the relationship between private credit markets and oil payments actually increased over time. Something in the description of "market forces working" suggests (per-

---

[29] See, for example, Solomon, *International Monetary System*, p. 314; Lomax, "Oil-Finance Cycle Revisited"; and Cline, *International Debt and the Stability of the World Economy*.

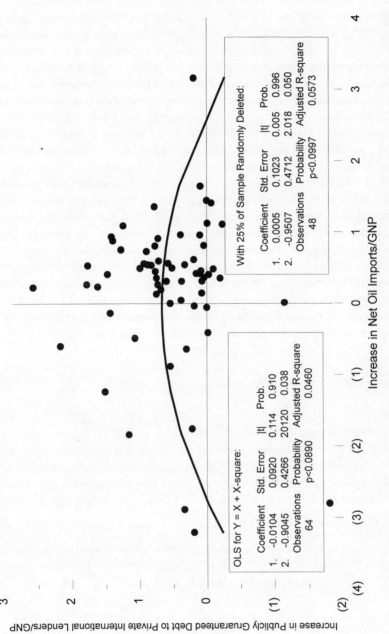

FIGURE 3.4. Increased credit from private lenders vs. increased net oil payments (1978–1981 increases/ 1978 GNP for each LDC).

With 25% of Sample Randomly Deleted:

	Coefficient	Std. Error	|t|	Prob.
1.	0.0005	0.1023	0.005	0.996
2.	-0.9507	0.4712	2.018	0.050
Observations	48	Probability p<0.0997		Adjusted R-square 0.0573

OLS for Y = X + X-square:

	Coefficient	Std. Error	|t|	Prob.
1.	-0.0104	0.0920	0.114	0.910
2.	-0.9045	0.4266	20120	0.038
Observations	64	Probability p<0.0890		Adjusted R-square 0.0460

Increase in Net Oil Imports/GNP

Increase in Publicly Guaranteed Debt to Private International Lenders/GNP

SOURCE: Debt and GNP figures from IBRD, *World Debt Tables* (various years). Oil figures from United Nations, *Yearbook of International Trade Statistics* (various years), country data for SITC 03. Random number table used to select second sample.

haps unfairly) that they reacted instantaneously to assist the world monetary system to adjust to a severe shock. Yet the increasing significance
over time tells us that there was a lengthy lag in their reaction time.
When we regress the debt figures for 1978–81 on the oil payments figures for 1973–78, the inverted U is more pronounced, at a higher confidence level, and with a greater adjusted R-square.[30] Again, the relationship between the two variables is significant but does not explain
much of the variance. It was likely during the 1978–81 period that
banks would lend to countries that did not increase the portion of income spent on oil, but it was even more likely if the countries had not
previously increased the portion of income spent on oil.

It is not accurate to say that market forces had nothing to do with
petrodollar recycling, only that markets did not intermediate between nations with oil surpluses and those with oil deficits. The prevalent view of
recycling takes as given the distribution of current account surpluses and
deficits and suggests that markets intermediated between the two. The
analyses above suggest the contrary. There does not seem to be much of a
correlation between credit flows and oil deficits, except insofar as banks
were less likely to lend money to nations with increased oil import bills.
International capital markets were not the primary conduit for balance-
of-payments adjustment financing after the oil shocks of the 1970s.

AN ALTERNATIVE EXPLANATION

The Mechanics of Recycling

Richard Mattione was among the first to point out that there was a
sharp difference between the current account performances of the
seven largest industrialized economies and the rest of the OECD.[31] Both
Mattione's and Paul Hallwood and Stuart Sinclair's studies also differentiate between NICs and low-income LDCs.[32] The advantage of divid-

---

[30] The independent variables were, first, an increase in net imports of crude petroleum
from 1973 to 1978 divided by 1978 GNP; and second, the square of the first variable (to
test for a quadratic function). The dependent variable was the increase in publicly guaranteed disbursed outstanding debt from 1978 to 1981 divided by 1978 GNP.

	Coefficient	Std. Error	$|t|$	P
1.	−0.3049	0.2425	1.257	0.213
2.	−3.0310	1.1500	2.636	0.011

Observations	Probability	Adjusted R-square
67	$p < 0.0118$	0.1023

[31] Mattione, *OPEC's Investments*, pp. 25–26. IMF annual reports had disaggregated industrialized countries into these two groups, but few scholars followed suit.

[32] Hallwood and Sinclair, *Oil, Debt, and Development*.

ing the world this way is that we then see there were four distinct groupings of nation-states with surpluses and deficits. If the world is divided
into three groups (industrialized nations, OPEC, and LDCs), recycling
explains how capital was transferred from OPEC to LDCs. When the
world is divided into four groups, we see that the mechanics of recycling
were considerably more complex.

For the nine years depicted in Figure 3.1, the Big Five ran a surplus of
$227.3 billion, while other industrialized economies had a deficit of
$142.6 billion. Industrialized nations were left with an overall surplus of
$84.7 billion. Non-oil-exporting less developed countries, on the other
hand, experienced a persistent and worsening trade deficit from 1973
to 1981. Exports of other industrialized nations to LDCs remained comparatively flat during the 1970s, but trade flows from the Big Five to
LDCs increased at an exponential rate.

One possible reason for the Big Five surplus to LDCs has nothing to
do with the oil shock or recycling. As Figure 3.5 shows, the exports of
manufactured goods by the largest industrialized nations have grown
exponentially for the past thirty years.[33] Figure 3.5 shows exports of the
Big Five in two categories of goods: all manufactured goods (excluding
two subcategories that represent raw materials) and SITC 7, which is restricted to machinery and equipment.[34] If Germany were to sell a knit-
ting machine to Korea, it would fall under this heading. Much of the
growth in exports of manufactured goods from 1965 to 1980 was accounted for by machinery and equipment. In turn, much of this growth
is accounted for by LDC imports.

In 1965, non-oil LDCs imported just 3.8 percent of all goods traded
in the SITC categories 5–8, and by 1980 they accounted for 8.9 percent
of manufactured imports. While the world share of non-oil LDC imports of manufactured goods doubled from 1965 to 1980, their share of
imports of petroleum products (SITC 3) remained nearly the same
(11.8 percent in 1965 and 11.7 percent in 1980). To present these data
in another way, manufactured goods were roughly half of all goods
traded in the world from 1965 to 1980. Though the portion of SITC
5–8 goods (out of all goods) varied between 50 and 55 percent, the
share of those manufactured goods imported by non-oil LDCs rose
from 14 percent (of all their imports) in 1965 to 23 percent in 1970 to
36 percent in 1980. Five newly industrialized nations imported $5 bil-

[33] Trade of manufactured goods is presented in the aggregate from all five industrialized nations to all other nations at five-year intervals.

[34] The categories are SITC numbers, which is how international organizations aggregate types of goods. SITC numbers 5 through 8 include most manufactured goods, and
SITC 7 is machinery and equipment.

FIGURE 3.5. Exports of manufactured goods by Big Five economies, 1965–1980 (US$ billions).

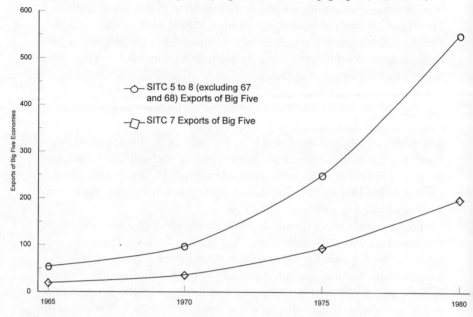

SOURCE: UNCTAD, *Handbook of International Trade and Development Statistics,* 1983, Table 4.1.

lion in machinery and transport equipment in 1970, and by 1980 that figure was up sixfold to $29 billion. This exponential growth is mirrored only by the exponential growth in private bank lending to NICs.

Industrialized democracies, competing with one another to bring their current accounts into balance, shifted the structural deficit onto NICs. The banks that were based in the industrialized democracies then lent money to the NICs to fund these deficits. To the extent that there was recycling, and to the extent that markets worked, it was in the sale of capital goods from the First to the Third World.[35] Recycling took place because the capital surplus in the First World was deposited in banks and lent to the nations that imported goods from the First World.

For this picture of recycling to be true, it must also be true that most bank lending went to NICs and not to all LDCs. In fact, that is precisely

[35] See Lewis, "Can We Escape the Path of Mutual Injury?" Professor Lewis argues that such lending constituted petrodollar recycling because the slowdown in trade was caused by the oil shock. The argument here is that such lending was indeed an indirect form of recycling, but because it was dependent on official assistance to other LDCs the bulk of recycling cannot be thought to have taken place through market forces.

what occurred. Lending went to only a very few comparatively rich LDCs, and the many other LDCs without access to private credit received capital from official sources.

Actors are defined and named by the attributes of their economies in an attempt at generalization. We do not say that Saudi Arabia deposited money with five banks, which then lent money to Brazil, because that would not tell us anything useful about the rest of the world. Yet the process of recycling was not radically different from this two-country description, and attempts to make it more general also have made it less accurate.

When "Brazil" was generalized to all LDCs, it aggregated the 150 nations of the Third World into one grouping, even though most of their debt was held by fewer than six countries. The Third World includes all of the OPEC countries and even some countries that are more developed than members of the European Union (EU). LDCs range from Bhutan, with a per capita GNP of $80, to Singapore (GNP per capita of $5,360). To speak of "LDC debt" when most of the debt is accounted for by a few well-off NICs is misleading.

In Figure 3.6 we see that Brazil, Mexico, and Algeria accounted for one-third of all credit to LDCs in 1973, 1978, and 1981.[34] Fourteen countries (almost all NICs and oil exporters) have accounted for more than 75 percent of all private lending to LDC governments since before recycling began. The same countries received roughly the same portion of all credit to LDCs before and after the two oil shocks. It is likely that the large GNPs of these countries, as well as their export-led development strategies, explain their share of credit. When lending to oil exporters and NICs remains more or less constant, regardless of oil shocks, then it cannot be true that such lending was spurred by oil deficits.

Figure 3.6 portrays stocks of credit, which is not a measure of new lending. Yet much the same results are obtained by comparing flows (increases in credit and net oil imports). Brazil, Mexico, Korea, and Venezuela received the four largest increases in private credit to LDC governments (roughly 50 percent of the total), while the next ten largest increases represented more than 25 percent of the total (and includes four oil exporters and four other NICs). The largest increases in oil import bills were borne by Brazil, Korea, India, and Turkey, and again this is best explained by their large GNPs. The less developed

---

[34] "All LDCs" refers to fewer than one hundred nations for which data are available. Nearly one-third of all LDCs are excluded from these figures because data are not available.

Figure 3.6. Publicly guaranteed LDC debt from private international lenders.

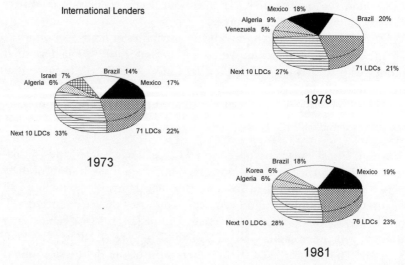

SOURCE: *World Debt Tables* (various years).

world is not one homogeneous unit, and the small number of NICs that received bank loans was not a representative sample.

While Brazil is a major borrower of private credit, and it is also a big consumer of oil, one did not cause the other. As Darrell Delamaide notes, "Latin-American countries began borrowing and defaulting as soon as they gained independence in the 1820s."[37] If there is one true and fast constant to be derived from the history of Latin America over the past two centuries, it is that Argentina, Mexico, and Brazil borrow money in London and then threaten to default. Such borrowing preceded the invention of the oil well by fifty years.

If the great majority of LDCs did not finance balance of payments deficits with private credit, they must have turned to official sources. As Figure 3.7 illustrates, this is precisely what happened. From 1976 to 1982 just six NICs accounted for 31 percent of the total non-oil LDC current account deficit, yet they accounted for 56 percent of all private capital to non-oil LDCs (the years 1976–82 were chosen solely because of the availability of data). The 130 countries that received the other 44 percent of private capital flows accounted for 95 percent of all official

[37] Delamaide, *Debt Shock*, p. 96.

JRE 3.7. Current account deficit financing in non-OPEC LDCs by source and country grouping, 6–1982.

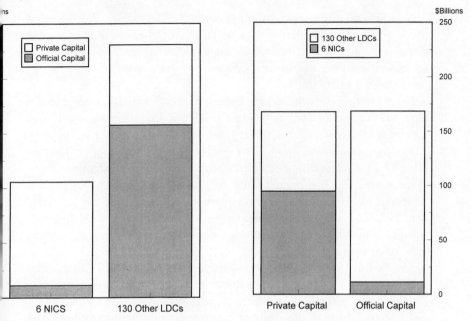

RCE: United Nations, *Yearbook of International Trade and Development Statistics*, Table 5.3, various years.

capital flows. Those other non-oil LDCs funded less than one-third of their current account deficits with private capital, while six NICs funded 90 percent of their deficits with bank loans and foreign investment. In this data series, some of the largest debtor nations are not included in the NICs group because they export oil. If such countries as Mexico, Venezuela, and Algeria were included, the contrast would be even more striking.

It is evident that the sources of the capital used to finance international trade deficits and the exporters' goods that made up those trade deficits were totally different. OPEC deposits in Eurobanks went to NICs to fund purchases of capital goods from the First World. Oil-related current account deficits in other LDCs were funded primarily by foreign aid from governments and international organizations. Some of that aid came from OPEC, but most of it was from OECD members. Thus the single most important source for the funding of oil-related current account deficits was the aid of industrialized nations.

The New Picture of Capital Flows

A revised picture of recycling is illustrated in Figure 3.8. It shows that there were two basic channels for recycling and that credit markets did not play the major role in establishing those channels. The new picture of recycling shows the arcane process by which capital made its way from OPEC to LDCs.

On the left side of the figure is the process in which banks played a part. OPEC made deposits in Eurobanks but also placed a significant part of its reserves with the governments of the five largest economies. Those five economies, which themselves had current account surpluses, joined OPEC in sending capital to Eurobanks. The banks lent money to many countries, but most of the loans went to newly industrialized countries (some of which were oil exporters). NICs, especially not those that export oil, did not spend that money on oil. They spent it on goods produced in the First World, which went to help increase their share in exports of manufactures.

On the other side of Figure 3.8 is the process by which LDCs financed their oil-related current account deficits. Some of the money came from OPEC, either directly in the form of bilateral aid or through organizations such as the IMF. The bulk of current account financing came from OECD countries. Many of these countries were capital-exporting economies in their own right, and more capital was deposited in their treasuries by OPEC surplus states. This new picture accounts for large bank loans to NICs and for global balance-of-payments data, and it explains the mechanics of current account financing for the LDCs that incurred an oil deficit.

In sum, although the prevalent view in the literature on the international monetary system holds that petrodollars were recycled from OPEC to LDCs by private credit markets, this does not appear to be the case. The new picture of recycling is consistent with all of the data, and there are several areas for which the prevalent view does not completely match up with capital flows in the 1970s.

Two main types of flows constitute the new picture of recycling. One is a flow of capital from OPEC and the five largest economies to banks, which lent much of the money to ten or so newly industrializing countries (including oil exporters). Those countries bought capital goods from the five largest economies, which contributed to their trade surplus. This flow of capital did nothing to alleviate current account deficits caused by oil price rises. It was a resting place for Arab capital but is recycling only in an indirect sense. The other channel of recycling

FIGURE 3.8. Capital and trade flows in recycling.

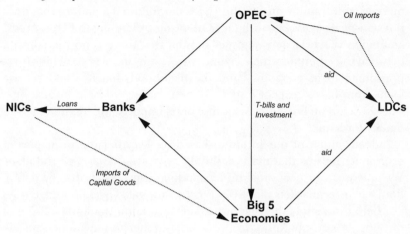

was the primary one for the specific purpose of getting money from surplus nations to those with deficits. This flow was official capital (foreign aid, IMF credit, and the like) from both OECD countries and OPEC members. The flows from OECD governments were made possible because the big five economies were capital exporters and also because of the very large amounts of capital the Arab surplus states placed with OECD governments (particularly the United States) in the form of treasury obligations.

The application of neoclassical economics to a disequilibrium in the global distribution of balance of payments is substantially different from what the prevalent view in the literature meant by saying that markets recycled petrodollars. In this chapter I found this view of recycling to be false by examining capital flows from both ends as well as the middle. At one end were the OPEC countries, and they did not put all of their money into banks (though they did put enough into Euromarkets to keep the average reader of this chapter content). At the other end of the transfer process were LDCs, and they did not fund their oil deficits by borrowing from banks. Indeed, the whole notion of OPEC being at one end of the channel and LDCs being at the other is not entirely accurate because many oil exporters are major borrowers from banks, and the five largest industrialized countries joined OPEC as net capital exporters.

In the middle of the putative process were the banks. Private credit markets grew rapidly during the 1970s but followed a pattern that does not statistically correlate with OPEC deposits or lending to LDCs. An examination of world debt statistics showed that there is no relationship between the extent to which a country was hit by increased oil bills (proportionate to its economy) and the likelihood that it would receive loans from banks, except insofar as the relationship is an inverse one. The worse off an economy is because of oil imports, the less likely it is to qualify for loans.

Indeed, much of our intuition based on learning the principles of economics tells us that markets should not have recycled petrodollars. Yet much of our economic understanding also tells us that by definition, whatever markets did was perfectly rational. This knowledge does not help us to study the role of markets in the international allocation of value. We do not know, for instance, whether the investment of billions of dollars by one government (Saudi Arabia) in the treasury obligations of another government (the United States) was economically rational or motivated by nonmonetary considerations. Should this exchange of value be called a market or a political deal?

Almost all literature on recycling carries the implicit assumptions of the neoclassical liberal school. Recycling occurred automatically through markets in which individual economic actors and states pursuing self-interests achieved a cooperative outcome. This came about, so this description goes, because oil-exporting states deposited their money in international banks, and those banks lent the money to countries facing deficits caused by the higher price of oil. In short, recycling was carried out by banks. The role of states was subservient to that of transnational financial firms.[38]

So pervasive is this view that otherwise astute observers do not question the conventional wisdom. Examples can be found in any almost any book that covers the recent history of the international monetary system. Even those writers who question the viability of basic assumptions about the smooth functioning of a liberal monetary system accept the neoclassical premise that surplus capital in one part of the world will find its way to finance deficits in other parts. Accordingly, Michael Moffitt writes:

[38] A few examples of this widely held view are found in Solomon, "Allocation of Oil Deficits"; Brown, *World Afloat*; Shultz and Dam, *Economic Policy beyond the Headlines*, esp. p. 92; IMF, *World Outlook*, June 1981; Tew, *Evolution of the International Monetary System*; and Aliber, *International Money Game*, 4th ed.

When a handful of oil-rich countries began to accumulate huge financial surpluses, the proceeds had to be recycled to oil consumers. Otherwise they would have been unable to afford OPEC oil and the world economy would have ground to a halt. OPEC dumped the funds in the Euromarket and the banks did the lending. Many of these loans were not traditional project loans, but went for balance of payments support. . . . Eurobanks took prime responsibility for the petrodollar recycling process.[39]

It is very surprising that the economists writing this version of recycling did not question their conclusions. To say that recycling went through banks does not make sense from either economic or political perspectives. There is no reason for banks to lend money to countries with continuing deficits unless the countries do not really need the money. Banks do not normally lend to uncreditworthy countries except under extraordinary circumstances. Thus it is likely that banks, given a sudden surplus of funds, would lend to industrialized countries, newly industrialized countries with strong export markets and little inclination to defend their current account, or oil-exporting countries with strong prospects for future income flows. It is unlikely (at least from the point of neoclassical theory) that the banks would experience a sudden inflow of new deposits after an oil shock. As William Branson points out, it was the depositors, not the deposits, that were new.[40] The money that went to pay for oil came out of savings accounts and went back into the banks as other nations' savings accounts. Neoclassical economics would posit that the financial transfer associated with a rise in oil prices involves little more than an accounting change in Western banks.

Proper use of neoclassical economics should lead to a view of recycling that was determined by the creditworthiness of deficit countries. Those countries unable to qualify for credit in a truly neoclassical world have had to adjust to the higher cost of an import by consuming less, working more, or both. Countries that could borrow would assume more of the oil-related trade deficit so long as the markets serving as financial intermediaries saw borrowing for balance-of-payments financing as temporary. This point was brought up by Paul Samuelson in the tenth edition of his textbook *Economics*:

The problem of "recycling" the tens of billions of dollars that each year accrued to the Persian Gulf countries represented a definite threat to world prosperity and to multi-lateral balance of payments equilibrium. . . .

[39] Moffitt, *The World's Money*, pp. 59 and 61.
[40] Branson, "OPEC Lending, LDC Growth, and U.S. Trade."

There still remains the problem of multi-lateral balancing: Suppose the excess oil revenues from selling to, say, India or Belgium are wished by the oil exporters to be held in U.S. bonds and stocks or U.K. bonds and stocks and not in Indian or Belgian assets. Will the U.S. be willing to lend to India and Belgium to make this all possible? Or, will Belgium and India be able to develop a favorable trade surplus with the U.S., thereby causing the whole process to balance out on a triangular basis? Clearly international cooperation is important here.[41]

For other neoclassical economists, the answer to Samuelson is that market forces should return international balance of payments to equilibrium. If the United States is not willing to lend to India, or if India is not able to develop a favorable trade surplus with the United States, then India will just have to import less oil. The Chicago school monetarist Harry G. Johnson put forth this view most forcefully when he compared nations to individuals:

Consider the question whether an individual faced with a rise in the price of gasoline for his car . . . must necessarily (i) borrow on distress terms or (ii) borrow in the specific form of running down his cash balance. Obviously there is no reason why he needs to run a balance-of-payments deficit (run down his cash balance) or resort to distress borrowing. He can instead sell assets in the market, reduce his rate of saving (asset accumulation), reduce his expenditure on other goods or work harder and earn more.[42]

Because governments could do the same as individuals—spend less or work harder—Johnson did not see an inherent necessity for higher oil prices to lead to balance-of-payments disequilibria. Therefore, he concluded, there was no need to mobilize international cooperation for the transfer of oil funds to deficit countries. "If the exercise of monopoly power is shameful, that is no reason why the conscience money should be paid by the monopolists to the most improvident and spendthrift countries."[43] Thus, while one noted economist has remarked upon the need for cooperation, and while consistent application of neoclassical theory leads us to understand that there might be a problem of cooperation, the popular view of recycling held by neoclassical economists

[41] Samuelson, *Economics*, p. 715.
[42] Johnson, "Higher Oil Prices and the International Monetary System," p. 166–67.
[43] Ibid., pp. 167–68.

(and shared by Johnson) is that market forces worked automatically to return the global balance of payments to equilibrium.

Economists do not draw the logical conclusions of neoclassical theory because doing so would challenge their underlying assumptions. They have a fundamental belief that harmony of interests is the principal dynamic on which the world works. Therefore, their description of recycling, contrary to facts and to their own theories, pictures a world in which the state is not important and actors cooperate with no external inducement.

CHAPTER FOUR

The Failure of International Institutions

Clearly, policy makers in the industrialized democracies agreed that the legitimate response to the oil crisis and to the challenges of recycling consisted of multilateral cooperation in international institutions and regimes. And an international institution responsible for balance-of-payments adjustment financing already existed: the International Monetary Fund. With the breakdown of the Bretton Woods agreement, however, nations sought other venues for cooperation. They engaged in economic summitry, made general agreements to avoid trade wars, and founded the International Energy Agency. Yet as this chapter shows, none of these institutions provided the cooperative outcomes predicted by liberal institutionalism.

In this chapter I consider the evidence for the liberal institutionalist thesis. I describe international summitry in response to the threat of competitive trade policies, the trade wars that followed, and the two failed attempts at policy coordination for petrodollar recycling in the OECD and the IMF.

SUMMITRY

Summitry by the industrialized powers in response to the oil shock is supposed to have been a precursor to the efficacy of functional regimes, and I will argue that it was a precursor to conflict. Two conferences in 1974 and 1975 led to the creation of the impotent and ineffective International Energy Agency. The Washington Energy Conference and the Conference on International Economic Cooperation were characterized by conflicts of interest. Openly expressing such conflict of interest did nothing to alter the international environment or the interests that were in conflict. If anything, self-contradictory statements by the United States and France, which made fairly clear their intention of pursuing selfish interests, exacerbated the rancorous atmosphere that pervaded in Atlantic relations.

It was to have been "The Year of Europe," according to the grand designs of Henry Kissinger. The year 1973 started with a series of disagreements between Kissinger and French foreign minister Michel Jobert. It ended with the North Atlantic Treaty Organization (NATO) and the European Community immersed in squabbles and with conflict extending to responses to the oil shock. As Kissinger wrote in his memoirs: "If France insisted on freedom of action in the Middle East, refused to participate in a consumer grouping on energy, and saw no point in any Atlantic declaration, little was left of the Atlantic dialogue."[1]

European perceptions of the problems posed by the oil crisis were different from those of the United States. The United States, like Europe, was a major importer of OPEC oil. As soon as the price of oil made difficult recovery profitable, however, there were vast reserves in the United States that could be (and were) developed. In a crunch, the United States would at least have some oil from domestic production. Europe was dependent to a much greater extent on foreign sources of crude petroleum.

Therefore, the United States with Kissinger at the lead favored a confrontational policy of forming a common front of oil consumers. He wanted to form a cartel of consumers that would lower the price of oil by acting as an oligopsony, much as the Seven Sisters had in past decades. European leaders preferred a more accommodationist approach to OPEC. No country ignored the danger of individual bilateral deals made between consumer nations and oil exporters. Yet by the same token, neither did any government ignore the benefits of secretly making such deals while other states cooperated to share the global balance-of-trade deficit held by oil importers.

These differences in perceived interests are explained parsimoniously by differences in geography and economic capabilities. Of all NATO countries, only those of North America depended on OPEC for less than one-third of their import needs. With the exception of West Germany (42 percent of energy imported from OPEC), Norway (47 percent), and Turkey (41 percent), the members of NATO depended

---

[1] Kissinger, *Years of Upheaval*, p. 278.

on OPEC oil for well over half of their total energy needs. This situation led the assistant secretary of state for European affairs, Arthur A. Hartman, to comment: "The figures suggest why European governments in varying degrees felt themselves hostage to Arab policies. In short, the European allies simply assessed their national interests in a different way than we did ours."[2]

This was the discordant background for what is commonly seen as the beginning of economic summitry. In January 1974, the Group of Twenty convened in Rome at the annual meeting of the IMF. The Europeans, particularly Dennis Healey, pushed for expansionary policies as a very general response to the oil shock rather than sharp adjustment through recession, but the United States would not agree.[3] Kissinger, rebuffed by the failure of the Year of Europe, wanted more than vague agreements on macroeconomic policy. He invited the six largest oil importers in Europe, Canada, and Japan to a summit of cabinet ministers called the Washington Energy Conference in February 1974.[4]

At the Washington Energy Conference more specific responses to the oil shock were discussed. Kissinger proposed a seven-point agenda for cooperation, which included conservation, emergency sharing, international financial cooperation on recycling mechanisms, and continued aid to LDCs.[5] Simon, while continuing Kissinger's theme of international cooperation by oil importers against OPEC, elaborated American plans for "Project Independence," which would enable the United States to become energy self-sufficient and no longer run an energy-related trade deficit. As other members of the conference pointed out, this independence would contradict the U.S. calls for cooperation. If the United States attempted to bring its trade into balance by becoming self-sufficient in oil, that would constitute precisely the type of unilateral policy that might end in a destructively competitive downward spiral.

The French response to this neomercantilist stance was more explicitly nationalist. Foreign Minister Jobert accused the United States of

---

[2] U.S. Congress, House, Committee on Foreign Affairs, *U.S.-Europe Relations and the 1973 Middle East War.*

[3] There was no written agreement among the countries to inflate their way out of the oil shock, and a source close to the British delegation said that Healey, who was slightly hard of hearing, left Rome under the impression that agreement had been reached. It was not until one year later, however, that most nations began fiscal expansion as an adjustment policy. Interview with Geoffrey W. Maynard, former chief economic adviser to Chase Manhattan, London, December 1984.

[4] Canada, France, West Germany, Italy, Japan, the Netherlands, Norway, and the United Kingdom. The secretary-general of the OECD was also invited, and Willy Brandt represented the European Community.

[5] Kissinger, *Years of Upheaval,* p. 906.

seeking international predominance rather than an end to the energy problem, and he implied that France would deal with Arab oil producers bilaterally. Walter Scheel, the German foreign minister, represented the European Community in refusing to engage in institutionalized cooperation among oil consumers. The foreign minister of Japan encouraged cooperation, yet at the same time he seemed to imply that his country would also pursue bilateral negotiations with oil producers.

Abject failure threatened the conference until Nixon spoke to the delegates during an impromptu after-dinner toast. He threatened that "security and economic considerations are inevitably linked and energy cannot be separated from either." The lure of isolationism was growing in America, he warned, and it would only be strengthened by European unilateralism.[6] The next day, the delegates (save France) agreed to a compromise. A relatively mild final communique called for increased cooperation through the OECD, but Jobert refused to go along.

France vetoed EC participation in future cooperation and insisted on inclusion of footnotes that said, "France does not accept point 9 [and similarly, 10, 16 and 17]." One point, to which France particularly objected, read: "In dealing with the balance-of-payments impact of oil prices they [the delegates] stressed the importance of avoiding competitive depreciation and the escalation of restrictions on trade and payments or disruptive actions in external borrowing." The other points to which France objected concerned future coordinating groups that would further discuss energy sharing and financial cooperation.[7] Kissinger later wrote, "The West was beginning to act like the old Greek city-states; by exalting self-will it dissipated its inspiration. The conference . . . would become *a symbol of our decline.*"[8]

Even without the discord between industrialized nations over how best to respond to the energy crisis (and as a secondary matter, the recycling problem), the vacuum of leadership in the United States, France, the United Kingdom, and Germany likely would have prevented any strong agreement. Edward Heath's government fell during the month of the energy conference, Pompidou died in April, Brandt resigned in a May scandal, and Nixon hung on until the summer. Yet by late the autumn of 1974 each of these liberal democracies had given the reins of power peacefully to a new leader. By September, discussion of an agreement between leaders likely to stay in power was again possible.

---

[6] Quoted ibid., pp. 915–16.
[7] Washington Energy Conference, "Final Communique."
[8] Kissinger, *Years of Upheaval*, p. 909, emphasis added.

There followed a brief period during which leaders were hopeful for co-ordinated action. But the hopes were not to be fulfilled.

Energy sharing was discussed at a meeting of the United States, Norway, Japan, Canada, and the EC (without France) in Brussels, and the tentative plans (had they been ratified) would have constituted an effective regime for reducing oil consumption and preventing shortages. The agreement called for stockpiling, emergency sharing, and coopera-tion in energy conservation. To overturn any action called for by the agreement, 60 percent of the votes were required out of 136 votes. Each of the thirteen member nations was to have 3 votes, and 100 votes were to be assigned by energy consumption. Thus the United States had 54 votes—3 as a member and 51 percent of the group's consumption of energy—which did not give it a unilateral veto but made it possible to veto any action with the acquiescence of just one other nation. The agreement was subject to ratification by each of the participating gov-ernments.[9]

Not one government even considered ratifying the agreement. France vetoed EC participation so long as the agreement constituted a consumers' cartel. The United States, therefore, delinked the issue of a financial safety net that was to ease balance-of-payments financing, and called for oil-dependent Europe and Japan to accept a current account deficit without coordinating a means by which to finance that deficit. It was an energy-sharing agreement initialed by low-level "sherpas," and it was for all of these reasons a nonstarter.[10]

In December 1974 the diplomatic deadlock was broken, but it cannot be said to have led to any sort of policy coordination. Schmidt, by then the German chancellor, convinced France to drop its veto and the United States to accept a non-confrontational dialogue with LDCs and oil producers. Presidents Ford and d'Estaing met on Martinique to con-summate the compromise, and the Conference on International Eco-nomic Cooperation (CIEC) was held in April 1975. "Nine months of ar-duous negotiations preceded the launching of the CIEC," testified the under secretary of state for economic affairs, and each point of conflict was resolved by broadening the issues to be discussed and the base of

[9] "News Conference at the Department of State by Thomas O. Enders, Assistant Secre-tary of State for Economic and Business Affairs," in Department of State, *Bulletin* 71, no. 1843, 21 October 1974; 525–33.

[10] At a May OECD meeting, however, member governments did agree to avoid unilat-eral measures and competitive depreciation for a period of one year. The agreement was not subject to ratification. The text of the agreement is reprinted in Department of State, *Bulletin* 71, no. 1827, 1 July 1974; pp. 32–33.

participants.[11] When the conference finally was held, it included twenty-six governments and split up into four separate commissions on energy, raw materials, development, and finance.

Because of the broad range of issues and the diverse interests of its participants, the Conference on International Economic Cooperation quickly turned uncooperative. In the words of the State Department, "talks were suspended." Clearly, the tortured and all-encompassing compromises reached by Ford and d'Estaing were responsible for the abject failure of the conference. There can be little dispute with de Menil's analysis: "The dynamics of give-and-take between the German Chancellor, the French President and the American President, which characterized the negotiations leading up to the Martinique agreement, was a harbinger of the way in which they were to use the summit process in subsequent years."[12] Of course, de Menil means this to be a testimony to the efficacy of international economic policy cooperation. I see the evidence as pointing to quite the reverse. Early summitry was character-ized by discord and paralysis. Faced with an economic shock that was it-self a result of the changing international distribution of economic ca-pabilities, industrialized nations were unable to reach meaningful agreements. Even with the United States attempting to impose its lead-ership, policy coordination had no efficacy. The evidence points not to the conclusions of de Menil and Solomon, but rather to the observation of Robert Putnam and Nicholas Bayne that "American leadership ap-pears to be a necessary, but not a sufficient, condition for summit co-op-eration."[13]

TRADE WARS

During the Rome meeting of the Group of Twenty in 1974, industri-alized nations agreed to pursue fiscal expansion in response to the oil shock and not to engage in beggar-thy-neighbor policies. Again in May, members of the OECD declared their determination

(a) to avoid having recourse to unilateral measures, of either a general or a specific nature, to restrict imports or having recourse to similar measures on the other current account transactions. . . .

[11] Statement of Charles W. Robinson, U.S. Congress, House, Committee on Interna-tional Relations, *International Economic Issues*, pp. 7–11.
[12] De Menil and Solomon, *Economic Summitry*, pp. 13–14.
[13] Putnam and Bayne, *Hanging Together*, p. 273.

(b) to avoid measures to stimulate exports or other current account trans-actions artificially; and inter alia, abstain from destructive competition in official support of export credit and aim at taking appropriate co-operative actions to this effect in the immediate future.[14]

While this high talk of avoiding unilateral adjustment took place, what were the largest industrialized nations doing? As can be seen from Figure 4.1, most were working very hard at unilaterally bringing their current accounts into balance. So contrary to stated agreements were the actions of the industrialized nations that members of the British economic policy establishment suspected that the leader of their delegation (who was slightly hard of hearing) had misunderstood what was said in Rome.[15]

With the United States at the forefront, the Big Five economies showed upswings in their balances on goods and services between 1974 and 1975. Germany ran a persistent surplus. The United States dropped to a deficit only during the Carter administration, and by 1979 it was in the black once again. These figures do not impute causation, but they do represent actions by the governments of industrialized nations to dampen demand for imports and expand exports. They would do so largely at the expense of smaller OECD members and LDCs.

Fiscal management of the "tradables sector" led to a chain reaction in defection from liberal economic relations.[16] A good example was the beggar-thy-neighbor policies of Italy. Those policies were a result of a reduction in German non-oil imports in 1974. Germany was Italy's biggest export market. The Italians borrowed from the IMF (and also from the West German government) and allowed the lira to depreciate sharply. As a result, the Italian balance on goods and services took a sharp hike north in 1975; and by 1977 it had joined Germany, Japan, France, and the United Kingdom as countries with surpluses on goods and services (it was in 1977 that the United States went into deficit).

Asked by a congressional committee in 1975 whether the Italians were not foisting their problems on the rest of the world, the economist Robert Z. Aliber pointed to the actions of the three largest industrialized nations:

[14] "Declaration Adopted by Governments of OECD Member Countries on 30th May, 1974," reprinted in Department of State, *Bulletin* 71, no. 1827, 1 July 1974; pp. 32–33.
[15] See note 3.
[16] Trade economists divide economies into tradables and nontradables. The division relates to what can and cannot be exported.

IGURE 4.1. Current account balances of the six largest economies.

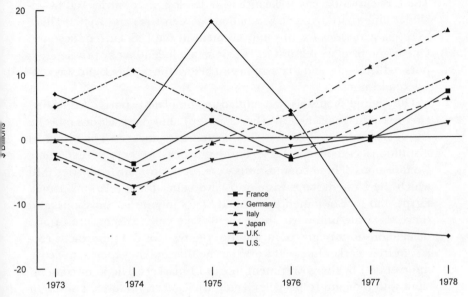

SOURCE: World Bank, *World Data 1995*, CD-ROM, line "BN CAB FUND CD" (current account balance after official transfers).

[Italy's depreciation] can be called beggar-thy-neighbor and I'm glad you raised that issue. There are three beggars in the world, and it's sad to say that the largest beggars are Germany, Japan, and the United States—beggars in the sense that in each of these countries, if we look at their trade balance developments over the last year, we find that their trade position developed much more favorably than was suggested by their increase in their oil import payments. They were throwing the problem of adjustment to the oil price increases onto other countries. Italy responded by allowing its currency to depreciate.[17]

Beggar-thy-neighbor policies in the years following the first oil shock were employed by the industrialized trading partners of the United States, but the United States did not sit by idly. In 1975, for example, the United States signed an agreement with the Shah of Iran to sell his

[17] Testimony of Robert Z. Aliber, U.S. Congress, Senate, Committee on Banking Housing and Urban Affairs, *Financial Support Fund*, p. 103.

nation $26 billion of military equipment and nuclear power plants.[18] The U.S. current account balance with developing countries (OPEC included) improved by some $12 billion between 1974 and 1976.[19] There were many reasons for this improvement in the U.S. current account. One of the primary reasons was the increase in lending by private creditors to LDCs—a trend that had begun before the oil shock and was considered legitimate.

The United States also attempted to stimulate exports "artificially" (in the language of the OECD declaration), and these actions must be considered a contradiction of legitimate trade practices. The principal institutions embodying these trade practices were Joint Economic Commissions. These commissions were set up in many countries with which the United States wished to have better trade relations. Israel, Egypt, and Jordan joined the United States in joint commissions, and there was little untoward about them. Like embassy-sponsored trade delegations to foreign countries, the commissions did not exactly represent free market forces at work, but neither did they represent active intervention by the government in export markets. The joint commissions with Iran and (especially) Saudi Arabia were, however, a different story.

In its first year, the joint economic commission with Iran had gained some $3 billion in future contracts for American firms. The joint economic commission with Saudi Arabia not only helped to procure contracts for American firms but provided for yearly meetings between the U.S. treasury secretary and the Saudi minister of finance. By 1981, the U.S. Treasury had collected more than $500 million from the Saudi government simply to fund feasibility studies for contracts given to U.S. firms.[20]

The joint commission was established in 1974 during a visit of the Saudi crown prince to Washington, and a formal and detailed agreement was signed in February 1975. The agreement called for a "Joint Commission on Economic Cooperation," to be headed by the U.S. treasury secretary and the Saudi minister of finance. It was to provide a forum for U.S. technical assistance and feasibility studies, and it also

[18] Testimony of Henry Kissinger, U.S. Congress, Joint Economic Committee, *U.S. Foreign Energy Policy*, p. 66.

[19] Preeg, ed., *Hard Bargaining Ahead*, p. 203.

[20] The account (number 20X6423) held less than $100 million in 1976 and grew markedly after 1979. Interview with an official in the U.S. Treasury, Washington, D.C., August 1983.

gave the two ministers of finance a chance to meet at least annually.[21] This commission differed from those set up in other Middle Eastern countries in three significant respects. First, it was assigned to the Department of the Treasury, whereas most other commissions were attached to the Department of State or the Department of Commerce. Since other commissions were primarily for providing technical assistance to less developed countries, they were put in the same department as the Agency for International Development. Commissions that were intended to increase trade with developed nations were attached to the Department of Commerce. Only the Saudi and Iranian commissions were assigned to the Treasury, and the reason was that their function was financial as well as commercial.

A second difference was the size of the Joint U.S.-Saudi Commission. Its staff grew to more than three hundred in Riyadh and Washington, and its annual budget grew to more than $2 million by 1981. According to a former director of the Office of Saudi Arabian Affairs in the Treasury Department (which was the only country-specific office in Treasury), the joint commission in Iran might have been just as big, "but it never really got off the ground."[22] A final difference is that the Saudi joint commission was the only one to serve as a forum for financial cooperation and for which there was an institutionalized meeting between ministers of finance each year.

Notably, in its first years it was funded by the Treasury Department's Exchange Stabilization Fund (ESF). The ESF was founded in 1934 as part of the Gold Reserve Act to manage balance-of-payments disequilibria in the United States. It was meant to be a standby coffer for alleviating severe disruptions in the international monetary system. By competing with other nations to sell goods and services to Saudi Arabia the United States did not stabilize the international monetary system, but it did stabilize its own current account.[23]

---

[21] "Technical Cooperation Agreement between the Government of the Royal Kingdom of Saudi Arabia and the Government of the United States of America," signed at Riyadh 13 February 1975, U.S. Department of the Treasury, TIAS 8072.

[22] Interview with Bonnie Pounds, Washington, D.C., 12 August 1983.

[23] The reason that the Treasury paid for the commission from the ESF was, however, probably less sinister. Treasury funding for the joint commission had not been submitted to Congress in the budget. Any extraordinary expenses in the Treasury Department that were not covered in the budget were often paid for out of the ESF because it was one of the few sources of funds for which Treasury officials did not have any public accountability. Treasury Department officials considered it simply a matter of bureaucratic expedience. Interviews with Theodore Rosen, commercial attaché U.S. Embassy (formerly in Office of Saudi Arabian Affairs, U.S. Treasury), Cairo, 7 February 1984; Bonnie Pounds,

A study by the General Accounting Office noted that the Joint Commission served as "an important mechanism for (i) fostering closer political ties between the two countries through economic cooperation, (ii) assisting Saudi industrialization and development while recycling petrodollars and (iii) facilitating the flow to Saudi Arabia of American goods, services and technology."[24] In each of these three aspects, the commission played a central role in unilaterally recycling petrodollars and fostering trade. More than twenty projects were begun under the auspices of the commission, all of which were to increase human resources in Saudi Arabia. The United States could not have found a more effective way to manage a transfer problem. By increasing the absorptive capacity of the country, the commission made it possible for all nations to export more to Saudi Arabia. Yet the commission, paid for in full by the Saudi government (ESF funds were reimbursed), did not make it easy for other nations to free ride. Feasibility studies done for the commission ensured that tender documents were geared to U.S. standards so that it was almost guaranteed that U.S. firms would win the contracts. In fact, the contracts not only went to American companies; quite frequently they went to American companies that had previously benefited from infusions of Saudi capital. The result was that the commission could draw Saudi investments to the American private sector by assisting the profitability of those investments.

With projects as diverse as the National Center for Financial and Economic Information, and Arid Lands, Meteorology, and Environmental Education, it was not unusual for more than one dozen offices and departments of the U.S. government to be involved in the annual meetings of the two ministers of finance. At its seventh annual meeting, in 1982, for example, the U.S. Departments of Treasury, State, Interior, Agriculture, Commerce, Labor, Transportation, and Energy were rep-

---

Washington, D.C., 12 August 1983; and Jerry Newman, treasury attaché (formerly head of Banking Office and head of Middle East Office, U.S. Treasury), London, 29 August 1984. All three worked in the Office of Saudi Arabian Affairs from its inception.

When Congress became aware that Treasury was using the ESF to pay Saudi nationals working for the joint commission, it passed PL95–61 prohibiting the Treasury from paying salaries from any source but appropriated funds. The point was not so much that the Congress disapproved of the joint commission as the danger that taxpayers would find out that they were funding technology transfer to a country that could not decide what to do with all of its capital. Yet the salient point was precisely that the Saudis were susceptible to advice on how to spend or invest their capital, and that was the primary function of the commission.

[24] U.S. General Accounting Office, "The United States–Saudi Arabian Joint Commission on Economic Cooperation," p. 2.

resented in Riyadh at no lower than the assistant secretary level. Yet the importance of these annual meetings, and therefore of the commission, was the informal (and off-the-record) agreements of the treasury secretary and the Saudi minister of finance.

At these meetings the United States was able to persuade Saudi Arabia to invest a sizable portion of its surplus in U.S. government obligations and to keep oil priced in dollars. And at the simplest level, it was at these meetings that the United States ensured that it would unilaterally bring its current account into balance with that of Saudi Arabia. The joint commissions were a focal point for American unilateralism. In their absence, American policies would have been largely the same. So these institutions represent ad hoc arrangements to further a foreign policy that consisted of bilateral actions.

None of these actions coincided with U.S. definitions of legitimacy; neither were they consistent with the international agreements signed by the United States. In this atmosphere, it is little surprise that nearly every industrialized nation broke its promise to avoid artificial stimulation of exports and incentives for capital inflows. It was a period marked by U.S. leadership: a form of leadership that increased the volition to defect from cooperative schemes.

THE SAFETY NET

While the United States was offering unilateral incentives to Saudi Arabia for capital flows, and while every industrialized nation pursued competitive trade policies, they continued to meet under the auspices of the OECD to coordinate policy on recycling. Kissinger's compromise with the French occurred at an OECD meeting, and the idea of coordinating recycling policy was intended to prevent competitive trade policies as well as to offer OPEC a multilateral investment fund so that it would increase oil production. As it turned out, however, the process of policy coordination did not produce a multilateral investment fund. The plans for recycling did maintain U.S. predominance. Although negotiations continued for several years, the idea of coordinated recycling never came to fruition.

To address his concern over the possibility of competitive trade policies, Kissinger proposed the establishment of a multilateral financial "Safety Net" that would guarantee developed nations the ability to cover their current account deficits. Because the Safety Net entailed an explicit commitment of funds by the United States, the agreement had to be presented to Congress in the form of legislation so that the funds could be appropriated.

Member nations of the OECD agreed to the Safety Net in 1975, and a bill to approve the Financial Support Fund (as it was formally known) was submitted to Congress that year.[25] The Safety Net had three primary functions. First and foremost, it was to serve as a lender of last resort for the international financial system. Second, it was to soak up OPEC funds from private markets and ensure that they found their way to countries with oil deficits.[26] Finally, it was an important principle that nations seeking access to Safety Net funds would have to agree to conditionalities. The purpose of these conditionalities was to prevent nations from pursuing competitive trade and beggar-thy-neighbor policies. Thus in Simon's public statements, the principles of the Safety Net were its temporary nature (as opposed to making it a part of an IMF Standard Drawing Rights [SDR] allotment), its role as an insurance fund, and the discipline that it would impose on its participants.

As an act of Congress, the Financial Support Fund bill defined the Safety Net as a "new international financial institution." Simon urged Congress to pass the bill: "The participation of the United States in the Support Fund will convey unmistakably our commitment to cooperation in preservation of a liberal and open world economic order—and it will do much to insure the result."[27] Undersecretary of State for Economic Affairs Charles W. Robinson put it in a similar light: "The cooperative spirit that has developed as a result of this oil crisis could be shattered by our inability or unwillingness to proceed with a commitment that we have already made to provide the special finance fund, the Financial Support Fund."[28]

In fact, though the Safety Net was presented as a continuation of international cooperation, it was a continuation of past economic relations only insofar as it gave an exorbitant privilege to the United States. If the Safety Net were not to be funded by Congress, America's partners in the OECD would have either to cut bilateral deals with OPEC surplus states or to tempt the fate of finicky international financial markets. Should they have chosen the former alternative, they would have found

[25] S. 1907, 94th Cong., 1st sess.

[26] U.S. Congress, Senate, Committee on Foreign Relations, *Financial Support Fund*, p. 180.

[27] Testimony of William Simon, U.S. Senate, Committee on Banking Housing and Urban Affairs, *Financial Support Fund*, p. 11.

[28] Ibid., p. 144.

themselves in direct competition with the New York Fed for Arab funds. Should they have chosen the latter—turning to the Eurodollar market—the majority might have (indeed they did) successfully funded their current account deficits, but by 1975 it was clear that Italy, France, and the United Kingdom would soon face unwilling private lenders.

A third alternative could have been a true cooperative solution—a Safety Net that did not give one state a blanket veto. But this alternative was not amenable to the United States. Instead, the Safety Net served to place the United States in between OPEC and the OECD as a financial intermediary with the power to veto loans unless a borrowing country agreed to conditionalities proposed by the Treasury Department. The Safety Net was thus compatible with the aims of the add-on policy and with Kissinger's policy of an IEA that confronted rather than cooperated with OPEC. It complemented the add-on policy because it allowed the United States indirectly to control recycling by taking surplus funds out of the market. It was confrontational because, as Simon noted,

> the support fund reduces the risk to the oil importers, the risk that they might be forced to accept onerous economic or political conditions as a price for needed financing. It frees the oil importers from a dependency that could weaken their resolve to the energy situation, which is a basic objective of the support fund. It would be anomalous to incite the exporters to help shape that response.[29]

Quotas in the Safety Net were assigned by calculations of international trade and GNP. The total was to have been twenty billion SDRs, which translated to about $24 billion in 1975. Each member could borrow its quota, subject to a two-thirds vote and agreement to conditionalities on free trade and fair exchange rates. With a 90 percent majority, a nation could borrow double its quota. This meant that the United States, with nearly 28 percent of the total quota, could veto any borrowing of more than a country had contributed. And with the agreement of any one of the next five largest contributors (or any two of the next fifteen largest), it could prevent a member from borrowing even its quota. The assigned quotas are presented in Table 4.1.

Plans for lending by the Safety Net were among the most interesting aspects of its design. Only after a member country requested assistance, agreed to conditions imposed by other members, and lending was approved by members with two-thirds of the total quota would the organi-

---

[29] Ibid., p. 9.

Table 4.1. Financial Support Fund quotas.

Countries	Percent of quota	Quotas (SDR millions)
United States	27.8	5,560
Germany (FRG)	12.5	2,500
Japan	11.7	2,340
France	8.5	1,700
United Kingdom	8.0	1,600
Italy	7.0	1,400
Canada	4.2	840
Netherlands	3.0	600
Spain	2.5	500
Belgium	2.4	480
Switzerland	2.0	400
Australia	1.5	300
Sweden	1.5	300
Denmark	1.2	240
Austria	1.0	200
Norway	1.0	200
Finland	0.8	160
New Zealand	0.8	160
Turkey	0.6	120
Portugal	0.6	120
Greece	0.6	120
Ireland	0.6	120
Iceland	0.1	20
Luxembourg	0.1	20
TOTAL	100.0	20,000

Source: U.S. Treasury Department.

zation borrow funds to lend to the member in need. Two options were available for provision of funds. The first was the ordinary mode of funding international organizations: member states would appropriate the funds in their own currencies and make them available to the borrower. The plans did not anticipate that this option would be taken unless financial markets were in complete disarray. The second option was for the Safety Net organization to issue securities backed by the full faith and trust of the member governments (in accordance with their quotas) in those markets where most OPEC capital had been deposited. In other words, it was a plan for redirecting capital from recalcitrant capital markets to nations with oil deficits. Since the vast majority of funds were denominated in dollars and deposited in U.S. banks (and their foreign branches), the Safety Net could potentially have bailed out American banks to a far greater extent than the U.S. quota represented.

The lending to the member nations was to be done at market interest rates for a period not exceeding seven years. Had the Safety Net been approved by Congress, it would have given uncovenanted benefit to American financial institutions and to the U.S. government, while helping deficit nations little more than minimally. The Safety Net simply formalized existing economic and political relationships between the United States and other OECD nations. It may have served as an incentive to the larger industrialized nations not to pursue competitive trade practices, but if the conditions had been that strict and effective, it is unlikely that the largest industrialized nations would have turned to it for funds.

In short, the Safety Net was a formalized arrangement of what by 1976 was the de facto mechanism for recycling. It was to absorb OPEC funds from U.S. markets and relend them under sovereign guarantees to nations with oil-related trade deficits. Those deficit nations would have to submit to the conditionalities and policies of an international organization in which the United States had veto power. Rather than being a multilateral investment fund or creating mechanisms for equitae sharing of OPEC capital, the Safety Net provided an ex post facto mechanism for recycling funds that the United States had attracted to its shores.

One might expect the strongest opposition to the Safety Net to have come from OECD members (other than the United States), but in fact, the final stumbling block was the American Congress. The European Community was not in dire need of current account financing by 1976 because most of its members already had pursued competitive trade policies. The nations that did require financing either turned to the Eurocredit market or made bilateral deals with OPEC nations—neither of which compelled them to accept U.S. conditionalities. And since the Treasury and State Departments had proposed the Safety Net as a counterpart to a consumers' cartel in the IEA, which never got off the ground, they were not anxious to force the agreement on Congress.

Congress in 1975 and 1976 was fighting unprecedented budget deficits, and it was reluctant to approve a request for $6.7 billion. The Financial Support Fund Act never made it out of committee, and by the time the Carter administration took office, it was clear that the votes simply were not there. With hindsight, had the act been passed it is not likely that it would have been a significant force in recycling because most OECD nations with oil deficits successfully turned to the private market for funds. The plans for the Safety Net, portrayed in the guise of international cooperation, however, show the unwarranted seigniorage that the United States attempted to derive by virtue of its dominant position in its economic relations with other nations.

THE INTERNATIONAL MONETARY FUND

When nations are in need of current account financing, or when the international monetary system faces challenges and change, the international institution given responsibility for addressing these problems is the IMF. Yet the possibility of policy coordination in the IMF was virtually ignored and in many instances thwarted by industrialized nations. The European ministers of finance who are credited with founding G-7 summits were uncooperative when the executive director of the IMF turned to them for a multilateral recycling facility, and the United States government directly competed with the IMF for Arab capital. This was not because of a lack of effort by the IMF staff.

Within ten days after OPEC announced its first large rise in the price of oil, IMF executive director Johannes Witteveen considered the options open to the organization he headed for recycling petrodollars. Like most analysts at the time, Witteveen and his staff did not believe that international financial markets could handle the recycling problem. Witteveen foresaw massive balance-of-payments deficits for the industrialized and less developed oil-importing countries and a massive surplus for OPEC countries with no established mechanism in place to effect the transfer of reserves from surplus to deficit countries.[30]

Because of the crisis atmosphere, raising quotas (which takes about two years because the member governments must approve such a raise) was out of the question. J. J. Polak, who was the economic counselor, favored a second option, which was to increase the allotment of Standard Drawing Rights. The purpose of increasing the allotment would have been analogous to a central bank pursuing expansionary policies to monetize a balance-of-payments deficit. If an increased allotment was to be an efficacious method for alleviating the oil-induced balance-of-payments problem, the surplus states would have had to be willing to hold SDRs, and they probably would not have liked the idea.

The principal stumbling block to increased allotment was the United States. In 1974 there had been a well-publicized White House conference on inflation. Because some Treasury officials likened an increased allotment of SDRs to expansionary monetary policy, even though SDRs were clearly not money, they vetoed the idea out of fears of increased world inflation. Both the U.S. director and the managing director's office felt that the balance-of-payments problems were temporary, and

---

[30] This section relies on interviews with Johannes Witteveen, Amsterdam, November 1983; and Andrew Crockett, Washington, D.C., August and September 1983. Additional material was provided by their staff.

therefore the solution should also be temporary. A telling criticism of the idea of increasing allotments was that it would be permanent. Witteveen turned to the third option: borrowing money for a temporary facility.

Borrowing was not new to the IMF by 1974. It had borrowed from the governments of Italy and Canada and under the General Arrangement to Borrow (GAB). Those loans were at 1.5 percent, which was far below the market rate by any standard. Witteveen did not think that he would have to pay market rates for the oil facility that he was about to create. Governments did not try to get real interest rates on loans to the IMF because, as a vice president of the New York Fed explained, "central banks are not out to make a fast buck off of the IMF."[31] Also, if the IMF was to pay market rates, it might eventually go to the market itself for funds, which would make it a supranational organization unfettered by the control that can be exerted over multilateral organizations by their dominant members.[32] The problem for Witteveen was to convince surplus states that they should act like the central banks of industrialized nations, even though they did not share the same power or interests.

Surplus states were to be the major creditor of the oil facility, but Witteveen hoped first to persuade one or two European powers to get the ball rolling by agreeing to participate in the lending. His trips to France and Germany, where he met with two finance ministers who were about to become prime ministers, were not successful. Though these two men are credited by de Menil as among the intellectual and policy-making founders of economic summitry and economic cooperation, Witteveen could not persuade them to cooperate with a pathbreaking initiative by the IMF.

He and his assistant Andrew D. Crockett also stopped in Geneva to talk with Ahmed Zaki Sa'ad, a retired executive director for Middle Eastern countries in the IMF. Sa'ad was an internationalist. He viewed his responsibilities as executive director as going beyond the particular interests of the Middle East.[33] Previously, Sa'ad had advised the Saudis to play a low-key role in the IMF because he felt that the onus of international

[31] Interview with Jeffrey Shafer, Washington, D.C., 16 September 1983.

[32] The IBRD does issue its own securities but is regulated in doing so by the vote of its members (and the United States has an absolute veto).

[33] Sa'ad was an Egyptian who had originally been nominated to his position by King Farouk. He retained his post until 1970, when he was appointed special ambassador for Saudi affairs in the IMF (he died in 1980). A staff member at the IMF recalled that "Zaki Sa'ad's name used to be talked about in the halls of the IMF in hushed whispers." He was said to have had extraordinary influence with the Saudi royal family, although by 1974 that influence was noticeably diminished.

monetary stability should be on the industrialized nations. The first governor of the Saudi Arabian Monetary Agency (SAMA) was Mu'ammar Ali, who was a former employee and protégé of Sa'ad (Ali named his first son after his mentor). Ali had established a policy at SAMA of isolationism from international monetary issues; and in 1974 SAMA did not have a tradition of contributing to international monetary stability. Witteveen wanted to convince the organization to change that policy.[34]

It was only natural that Witteveen would try to convince Sa'ad of his scheme before visiting the Middle East, but the meeting did not go well. Witteveen and his aide almost failed to recognize Sa'ad in Geneva's Continental Hotel. "He shuffled around in an old overcoat that made him look like one of the cleaners," Crockett recalls, "and he mumbled into his chin." Witteveen also remembers that meeting as one of the most humorous events during his tenure at the IMF. "Sa'ad always used to mumble in a thick accent. I didn't understand a thing he said." Engaged in an important act of international monetary diplomacy, Witteveen was unable to admit that he had no idea what had transpired during the half hour meeting, and aides of the two men had to reconstruct the conversation. After what Sa'ad had been mumbling about emerged, it became clear to Witteveen that Arab governments would not likely lend funds to the IMF unless they were paid market interest rates.

One month later Witteveen set off on another trip to the Middle East. After a two-day trip to Algeria, where Witteveen paid respects to Col. Houari Boumedienne (the spokesman for radical Arab states), he flew to Riyadh. By then Witteveen realized that any loans to the IMF would be well above the 1.5 percent interest paid on GAB loans, but still he hoped for an element of concessionality. During his first meetings in Riyadh he suggested an interest rate of 5 percent, "and that idea was rather quickly scotched."[35]

His sales pitch basically rested on the merits of international responsibility. "It is in your interest [to loan the IMF money]," he told them, "because you want to maintain a healthy international economy. It is in your interest because you have to have somewhere to put the money, and the IMF is a secure place. If you lend it to the Fund it is guaranteed."[36] The pitch was not only to lend to the Fund but to lend at one-quarter to one-half of a percent below LIBOR (the London Inter-Bank

---

[34] Indeed, when Richard Debs first visited Saudi Arabia as a vice-president of the New York Fed in 1972, many officials at SAMA did not know what the Fed was. Interview with Richard Debs, New York, 14 September 1983.

[35] Crockett, interview.

[36] Witteveen, interview.

Offered Rate). Some bargaining took place, but once the Saudi King had decided that the loan would be made, the negotiations simply involved getting the best possible deal. In the final count, the Saudis were comparatively forthcoming.

Witteveen's lecture on international responsibility and the security of an investment was by no means the first time such arguments were presented to the Saudis. By the time the IMF had gotten there (in April 1974) a line of central bankers, finance ministers from LDCs, and presidents of major financial institutions had already been through Riyadh. The reminiscences of Andrew Crockett, Witteveen's aide on the trip, illuminate the extent of sudden competition for Saudi funds:

> We [the IMF delegation] got special treatment. Three of us from the Fund shared a room in a rundown hotel with cockroaches and bedbugs. I had a cot, and that was high-level treatment. If you were just a regular president of a bank you had to rent a cab and sleep in the back seat for a hundred bucks a night. . . . It's just a trivial story, but seeing a string of bedraggled presidents of banks coming hat in hand must have had an effect on the relatively junior people [in SAMA] we were dealing with.[37]

The IMF had come up with a figure to suggest to each major surplus country, rather than just "rattling the cup and ask as much as you can."[38] The figures were determined on the basis of oil export levels and absorptive capacity. The figure suggested to Saudi Arabia was $2 billion, and the IMF delegation came away from Riyadh with $1.2 billion at one-half of 1 percent below LIBOR.

Now that it was established that the Fund was to borrow at just below LIBOR, Witteveen did not anticipate problems in getting loans from the other OPEC countries. Under the GAB, loans to the IMF were somewhat akin to a tax, with the resultant free-rider problem. With loans at near market rates, support for the oil facility was neither a tax nor an uncovenanted benefit to those who did not participate. Nonetheless, Witteveen had a "frosty reception" in Kuwait. His sales pitch to the Kuwaiti minister of finance al-Atiqi was greeted with a speech straight from Shylock in *The Merchant of Venice.* "When we come to Europe you spit on us because we are Arabs," said al-Atiqi, "and now shall we give you our money?"[39] In spite of al-Atiqi's identification with an anti-Se-

[37] Crockett, interview.
[38] Ibid.
[39] The original line (Act I, Scene 3) was "You call me a mis-believer, cut throat dog / And spit upon my Jewish gabardine / . . . Well then, it now appears you need my help." I thank Mrs. Bernard I. Heller (personal correspondence) for pointing this out.

mitic Shakespearean stereotype, Kuwait did participate in the oil facility. Many other OPEC members did not. Venezuela "eventually did, in extremely bad grace,"[40] but Algeria, Nigeria, Indonesia, and Iraq did not. These countries were soon to become recipients of "recycled" funds from the Eurodollar market.

The oil facility and its successors were to play relatively unimportant roles in the recycling of petrodollars, both in volume and influence. As the embodiment of the international cooperative regime for monetary stability and readjustment of global current account imbalances, it is not unreasonable to expect that the IMF should have provided a cooperative solution to recycling if any meaningful cooperation is to be expected in the future. Yet at nearly every step of the way, IMF policies were blocked by the United States. Witteveen felt that he was in direct competition with the U.S. Treasury for Saudi funds, and he felt further that the relative insignificance of the oil facility was the result of U.S. competition. Not only did the IMF have to pay more than the United States for the use of Saudi funds, it also had to get U.S. approval for all of its actions.

Under rules established for the GAB, a major lender to the IMF is given its own executive director. This meant that Saudi Arabia had a much greater vote than it would have from its SDR allotment alone. During the same period, the Peoples' Republic of China was recognized by the IMF, and its SDR allotment was raised, thereby threatening the U.S. ability to cast a blanket veto on any vote. After its first loans to the IMF, Saudi Arabia insisted on having its own director in accordance with IMF rules if it were to make further loans.[41] The American delegation disputed Saudi Arabia's right to a director and called for new voting rules that enabled the United States to retain its blanket veto with a smaller proportion of IMF votes. Only when its veto was preserved did the United States agree to new IMF borrowing from Saudi Arabia. In short, as U.S. votes in the IMF declined—reflecting its declining economic position—the United States blocked cooperative solutions until its dominance was reestablished.

The narrative of Witteveen's efforts to institute a recycling facility demonstrates the difficulty of mobilizing international coordination in the absence of a strong leader. Because the United States was unwilling to support the oil facility, it was relegated to minor importance in the global scheme of recycling. Although the United States participated

[40] Crockett, interview.
[41] Interview with Samuel Cross, New York, 20 September 1983; and Samir el-Kouri (of the Saudi delegation to the IMF), Washington, D.C., September 1983.

more actively in the IMF during the Carter administration, its early re-luctance to support the international institution that it had itself cre-ated is of great significance. So long as the process norms of the IMF gave weight to a nation's relative economic capability, the declining United States had little reason to assist the IMF in gaining a greater scope of responsibility in international adjustment. Only when the process norms were changed (i.e., the United States maintained its veto power with fewer votes) did American policy makers accede to the min-imal recycling done by the IMF.

U.S. policy toward the IMF raises two important points. The first is that the United States, as it declined in the 1970s, sought to alter the function of the IMF, which made it less cooperative and less able to bring about coordination absent the sponsorship of the United States. The second point is that U.S. actions in the IMF clearly illustrate the general U.S. strategy, which was to alter the political boundaries of in-ternational markets so that they would again produce the outcomes that favored the United States before the oil shock. And if an international regime stood in the way of this strategy, the simple response of the United States was to compete with it.

Cooperation was not the outcome either in the specific institutions for petrodollar recycling or in the broad regimes for macroeconomic policy coordination. Industrialized nations recognized the situation as a dilemma of collective action, and each one responded by defecting. In the realm of economic summitry, relations were characterized by acri-mony and self-interest. The regime created specifically for petrodollar recycling—the Safety Net—was little more than a reification of Amer-ica's fading dominance over Europe and a post-hoc codification of what was already taking place. Yet even this modest regime was nixed by the U.S. Congress.

The obvious regime for balance-of-payments adjustment financing was the IMF, but the United States prevented it from taking a major role in the process. By preventing the IMF from taking on greater responsi-bility, American leadership helped to dismantle the efficacy of a fading regime.

International institutions had many opportunities to contribute to re-solving the challenges of petrodollar recycling. They had almost no im-pact on the final outcomes. There is no evidence that these institutions altered the environment by lowering transaction costs, providing infor-mation, or making policies more transparent. Indeed, there is little evi-dence that the initial problems they faced were analogous to market failure. Almost nothing in the institutionalist literature is confirmed by this case study, which was one of the most crucial crises in modern economic history.

So is this case a proper test of liberal institutionalism? Perhaps not. Statespeople mouthed desires for cooperation, but there seemed to be real and enduring conflicts of interest. Perhaps this is not the sort of case that liberal institutionalism seeks to address. But if liberal institutionalism cannot address an important case in which existing and proposed international institutions failed to act (or were prevented from acting by American policy), then perhaps the theory is a bit too marginal to be of utility to the general study of international relations.

CHAPTER FIVE

Competing for Capital

Chased by a Roman army, his back to the North Sea, a Bretton general complained about Roman rule. "To plunder, steal, and rapine, these things they falsely call imperial rule. They make desolation and they call it peace."[1] Interpretation and rigorous argument are necessary to differentiate between peace and making desolation.

This chapter traces the unilateral policies pursued by the United States during the course of petrodollar recycling. Unilateralism began with U.S. policies that prevented the IMF from taking a larger role and ended with a nominally "multilateralist" administration that continued the United States's policy of diminishing the efficacy of international institutions.

COMPETITION WITH THE IMF

The International Monetary Fund allocates voting power according to who contributes how much money, and it decides on changing the allocation of contributions by voting.[2] For votes on issues that will funda-

---

[1] Tacitus, *The Agricola*, chap. 30, line 15.

[2] Unless otherwise noted, the material for this section comes from interviews with Johannes Witteveen (former IMF managing director), Amsterdam, November 1983; Andrew Crockett (formerly Witteveen's assistant), Washington, D.C., 17 August and 15 September 1983; Samuel Cross (formerly of the the U.S. delegation to the IMF), New York, 20 September 1983; Samir el-Kouri (of the Saudi delegation to the IMF), Washington, D.C., September 1983; and David Mulford (formerly of SAMA), Princeton, New Jersey, 1983. Because so much of the interviews concerning the Saudi compromise with the IMF was off the record, I do not attribute specific points to specific interviews.

mentally affect the distribution of power in the IMF, a "high majority" of 85 percent is required (and before 1978 it was 80 percent).[3] In 1978, when the effective veto dropped from 20 to 15 percent, the U.S. voting share fell just below 20 percent for the first time in IMF history.[4] The U.S. quota has fallen from 30 percent in 1949 to 25 percent in 1959 to its present level of 19.52 percent.

The veto changed in 1978, with the Sixth Review. That review was supposed to have taken place in 1974, but it was delayed by the United States. It was obvious that the voting shares of OPEC nations would have to be increased, and this implied that the United States would lose its veto. Therefore, the United States held up the review for four years until the high majority was reduced.

In the meantime, IMF director Johannes Witteveen put together the second oil facility with lenders from both industrialized nations and OPEC. SAMA was the major contributor, lending 34.8 percent of the funds. Many other non-OPEC nations contributed to the oil facilities. The United States did not.

This reluctance carried over to the Seventh Review of Quotas and to the Witteveen facility (formally, the Supplemental Financing Facility). Another voting rule directs that if the IMF uses a currency of a nation that is not one of those with the five largest quotas (i.e., not the United States, United Kingdom, West Germany, France, or Japan), then that nation may appoint an executive director for a two-year term.[5] Canada appointed a director in 1958 based on this provision, and Saudi Arabia did so in 1978.[6]

The issue in the allocation of quotas in the Seventh Review was once again how much the Saudis would be allowed to increase their voting share while increasing the amounts of capital they lent to the IMF. To the extent that the United States agreed to supplemental financing for the IMF, it wanted to see resources provided by borrowing capital from OPEC. That way, OPEC would not have any permanent position in the IMF, and when the loans were repaid the Saudis would have to relinquish their directorship. The Saudis, however, wanted as high a quota as possible so that their voting position would not always depend on loans.

The compromise solution was linked to two issues. First, the United

---

[3] Gold, *Voting Majorities in the Fund.*

[4] Solomon, *International Monetary System*, pp. 282–83.

[5] Southard, *Evolution of the International Monetary Fund.*

[6] The U.S. delegation did not formally recognize the right of the Saudis to appoint a director because the IMF rule says "currency," not "country," and the Saudis lent the IMF U.S. dollars, but the U.S. delegation did not formally object.

States agreed to a large increase in the Saudi quota at the same time that the Saudis dropped the idea of pegging the price of oil to the SDR. The U.S. quota was also raised so that it retained its position relative to other countries (i.e., its vote remained at just below 20 percent). This was an important concession to the United States because the Saudi quota was raised by 350 percent at the same time that China was given a new role. China had inherited the quota of what the IMF now recognizes as the "Province of Taiwan," and that quota was now raised by 327 percent. With the new quotas, Saudi Arabia had moved to the sixth largest member of the IMF (it was the thirty-eighth largest until the Sixth Review), and China was ninth. Significantly, the quota of Kuwait was increased but its voting position remained almost the same, and Iran was not given any increase.

Thus an important part of the compromise was to give Saudi Arabia more voting power so long as the United States did not lose voting power and so long as the Saudis prevented OPEC from shifting the price of oil out of dollars. Within the IMF, there was another part of the compromise. Saudi Arabia agreed to contribute heavily to the Witteveen facility, but Witteveen had to finance at least half of it with capital from industrialized nations. By continuing to lend the IMF funds (and at near market rates) the Saudis were able to appoint an executive director. In short, the Saudis had to lend the IMF money and keep oil priced in dollars in exchange for a change in voting rules. This compromise was made necessary by U.S. reluctance to see the International Monetary Fund it had created grow more powerful as the United States declined.

The Add-on Arrangement

In July 1974, an economic analyst at the CIA (he later worked for the Treasury Department) wrote a report titled "Problems with Growing Arab Wealth," which stands out years later as the best analysis of the recycling problem to date. The author of the report argued that markets would have difficulty handling so much money at once and that in any case they would not recycle it efficiently enough to prevent restrictive trade policies. More petrodollars would come to the United States than any other country because of its large and highly liquid capital markets. The problem was that if money flowed naturally to U.S. capital markets, the United States would bear the brunt of the global trade deficit with OPEC, because those same markets would not be likely to recycle the capital to nations with balance-of-payments difficulties.

Relevant portions of the report are presented here because it had an impact on policy and because only heavily edited versions have been published to date. Portions that have not been declassified (and therefore not published) are emphasized in italics:

Numerous proposals have been made to modify the financial structure to better accommodate and recycle the massive inflow of Arab funds. The suggested options fall into two broad categories:
—Those in which multilateral organizations circumvent the market by directly attracting and recycling Arab funds to consuming nations.
—Those in which official financial institutions, primarily central banks and treasuries, assist the market in attracting and recycling Arab funds. . . . (p. 12)

Only a few national markets will be able to attract Arab funds even if special financial or other incentives are offered. *As a result, because of the size and depth of the U.S. financial market, it will still receive the largest share of Arab investment, even if no special incentives are offered.*(p. 16)

Consumer countries could more favorably finance higher oil prices and maybe avoid restrictive trade measures or stringent deflationary policies designed for a quick current account adjustment. Countries providing new arrangements to facilitate financing of oil-related current account deficits could incur substantial net interest costs, but they would probably be smaller than the costs incurred under alternative options. *By incurring a larger share of the financing costs, the countries* providing special arrangements would facilitate gradual and less disruptive adjustment to higher oil import bills. (p. 17)

National financial markets, as they now stand, are not well suited to recycle surplus petrodollars. Many oil consumers will be unable to borrow enough on acceptable terms to finance their oil-related deficits.

New arrangements could facilitate recycling. Because of the immensity and offerings of its financial market, the U.S. could become the "entrepot" for Arab capital until the Arabs are willing and able to invest their surpluses in a large number of national markets. Although the U.S. could incur some costs in supporting lending to consuming countries on concessional terms, the U.S. trade deficit may be less because other countries would be prone to adjust and redistribute more gradually their non-oil current account deficit.(p. 19)[7]

Right before this report was written, Treasury Secretary William Simon's office was hard-wired for classified cables from the CIA. Simon

---

[7] Central Intelligence Agency, "Problems with Growing Arab Wealth," ER-IR 74-19, July 1974. A declassified version is reprinted in U.S. Congress, House, Committee on Government Operations, *Federal Response to OPEC*, part 1, pp. 863–81.

denied in an interview that he made much use of the CIA analysis, but during the same interview he did not recall such details as the names of his top aides, so it is possible that he has forgotten.[8] The CIA installed the machine because cable traffic to the Treasury Department had increased dramatically, and it was becoming increasingly onerous for the CIA to send reports via messengers with clearance. The intelligence agency also found it burdensome to ensure that the reports went only to those Treasury officials who were cleared to see them. For these reasons, the machine was installed in Simon's suite of offices. It was impossible for the CIA to know just how carefully Simon read the reports. Circumstantial evidence suggests that he did read them and that he heeded them as well.[9]

In July, William Simon made a trip to the Middle East, the highlight of which was his stop in Saudi Arabia. There he completed an agreement to offer the Saudi Arabian Monetary Agency an "add-on" arrangement, by which the United States government undertook to sell SAMA treasury obligations outside of the normal auctions held by the New York Fed. This was not the only agreement that Simon reached with the Saudis, and, indeed, his trip represented a culmination of previous negotiations.

In April, the United States and Saudi Arabia had announced jointly an upcoming visit by (then) Crown Prince Fahd to Washington. The announcement noted that "the two countries are prepared to expand and give more concrete expression to cooperation in the field of economics . . . and in the supply of the Kingdom's requirements for defensive purposes."[10] During his visit on June 8, Fahd announced the establishment of a Saudi Arabian–United States Joint Commission on Economic Cooperation. Financial cooperation was discussed in broad terms.

Richard Nixon, besieged by his accusers in Washington, left the United States for a trip to more friendly locales that same month, with stops in Saudi Arabia, Egypt, and Israel. Overwhelmed by the Watergate scandal, Nixon was not in a position to conduct foreign policy. It is not likely that he negotiated any aspects of recycling with Saudi royalty, but it is fairly clear that by the time of his visit the idea of Saudi investment in the United States had been firmly implanted in the agenda of U.S.-Saudi relations. By the time of Simon's visit the following month, only

---

[8] Interview with William Simon, chairman, Wesray Corporation (formerly secretary of the U.S. Treasury), New Jersey, 22 September 1983, by telephone from Washington, D.C.

[9] Interview with CIA station chief, Cairo, January 1984.

[10] State Department Press Release, "United States and Saudi Arabia to Expand Cooperation," no. 133, 5 April 1974.

the details needed working out. The view of a National Security Council staff member was that "Kissinger was running the show," but bargaining over details was considered unseeming by the Foreign Service. Thus the details were left to Treasury—and Treasury staffers shared none of the hesitancy to negotiate details.[11] In the words of a National Security Council official (to be echoed years later in the Contragate hearings), "We were dealing with leading rug merchants."

Accompanying Simon were Jack Bennett (under secretary for monetary affairs) and Gerald Parski (assistant secretary), who handled most of the details concerning sales of T-bills. A logical person to have discussed T-bill sales would have been the vice-president of the New York Fed's Foreign Department, but when Board of Governors chairman Arthur Burns found out about Richard Debs's intentions "he blew his top," even though Debs had made previous trips to Arab capitals.[12] In fact, Burns seems to have represented the sole faction of the U.S. government to express reservations about the recruitment of Saudi funds. Every other branch of the government was fairly enthusiastic about the policy.

Burns's reservations stemmed from his annoyance at attempts by New York Fed officials to reassert their position as the part of the Federal Reserve System responsible for international banking. Since the 1920s, the New York Fed had been declining in importance. The need for recycling gave the New York Fed an opportunity to return to its former glory, and Burns wanted to prevent that. If the bulk of Arab funds were to be placed with the New York Fed, Burns's strategy of centralizing Federal Reserve functions in the Board of Governors would be weakened. So Debs did not go to the Middle East in July 1974, but the New York Fed did receive the responsibility it sought.

---

[11] Interview with Doug Feith, Washington, D.C., 19 August 1983.

[12] Interview with Richard Debs, New York, 14 September 1983. Simon does not remember inviting Debs on the trip, and he disputed the idea that he would have sided with a New York Fed vice-president against Arthur Burns. Samuel Cross (a New York Fed vice-president and formerly deputy assistant secretary in the Treasury Department and executive director of the IMF) also downplays the importance of Debs's role. Interview with Samuel Cross, New York, 20 September 1983. Nevertheless, the idea of a bureaucratic alliance between the New York Fed and the Treasury Department against the Board of Governors was mentioned by several bankers and officials of different government departments. Interviews with Harold van B. Cleveland, vice-president, Citibank, New York, 22 July 1983; Michael Palmer, president, Associated European Capital (formerly president, Arab Investment Corporation), New York, 21 and 23 September 1983; Jeffrey Shafer (New York Fed), Washington, D.C., 16 September 1983; and Joseph Twinam, director, Foreign Service Institute (formerly on Arabian Peninsular Affairs Desk and ambassador to Bahrain), Washington, D.C., 18 August 1983.

Overall, the purpose of Simon's trip was to "buddy up with the Saudis."[13] Saudi cooperation was needed on many fronts, and Simon wanted to avoid the appearance of begging for money. Accordingly, the portion of Simon's briefing book that described recycling was small relative to the whole. Most of the negotiations concerned alleviating Saudi development bottlenecks (manpower and technology) so the country would import more in the future. Yet a significant part of the high-level negotiations concerned the add-on arrangement.

Quite simply, the add-on arrangement allowed the Saudi Arabian Monetary Agency to buy U.S. government obligations without competitive bidding. The average price they paid, however, was only marginally cheaper than the average price private firms paid. Normally, when the Treasury announces how much and what types of debt it wishes to sell, the Federal Reserve Bank of New York takes sealed bids from a select group of securities firms. The amount of government debt that each firm receives depends on the price it bids. This allocation of securities is called a competitive tranche. Smaller firms (and individuals) are permitted to purchase debt in a noncompetitive tranche, which means that they promise to buy a certain number of securities at the average price determined by the competitive tranche. Both the large firms and individuals can then resell the securities on the secondary market. The price on the secondary market usually reflects the average price bid at the Federal Reserve auction.

Under the add-on arrangement, SAMA was able to buy securities at the average price (as determined by the competitive tranche), but outside of the auction. These issues of securities were supplemental to the normal parcel of debt offered at auction. The Treasury was therefore able to lower the amount of debt it put up for sale at auction (which should have meant its debt fetched a higher price), but since the additional debt would have been bought by a single bidder (SAMA) and not by the other auction participants, the price as set by supply and demand should not have changed.[14] The only effect on the price of Treasury issues would have been related to the number of bidders at the auctions. According to formal theory, the final selling price in an auction is marginally lower as the number of participants drops by one.[15] None of the policy makers in the Treasury or the investors in SAMA interviewed for

---

[13] Interview with Theodor Rosen, commercial attaché, U.S. Embassy (formerly in Office of Saudi Affairs, U.S. Treasury), Cairo, 7 February 1984.

[14] See Mattione, *OPEC's Investments*, pp. 68–70.

[15] Bids are based on an actor's utility (i.e., the highest price she is willing to pay) and the number of participants. The bid price is given as $U^*(n\text{-}1)/n$.

this book were aware of the theory. Yet all saw an advantage to the Saudis in the arrangement.

Final details of the add-on arrangement were worked out in December 1974. According to a Treasury memorandum sent to Kissinger (reprinted as Figure 5.1), SAMA would purchase some $2.5 billion of new Treasury issues with a maturity of one year or more through the New York Fed. The $2.5 billion would be in addition to any other government securities that SAMA wished to purchase, either through the Fed or through private channels. If SAMA wished at any time to sell the securities, it promised to notify the Fed in advance, and the U.S. government would have first option at repurchasing the debt at prevailing market rates. In addition, the Treasury promised to consider selling SAMA nonmarketable securities. The memo concluded "The *sine-qua-non* for the Saudis in this arrangement is confidentiality and we have assured them that we will do everything in our power to comply with their desires."

The add-on arrangement was beneficial to the U.S. government for two reasons. First, and most obvious, it gave the government access to a huge pool of foreign capital, which eased the effect of Treasury borrowing on domestic capital markets. To the extent that Treasury borrowing was "crowding out" private investment, the Saudi capital would help both the government's finances and the domestic economy in general. A second advantage for the U.S. government was its ability to control inflows of Saudi capital by putting SAMA investment on a central bank to central bank basis. The most efficient way to do this would have been to offer "specials," which are illiquid securities that cannot be sold to anyone but the Fed.

In October 1975, officials in the Treasury Department proposed just such a debt offering to SAMA. These debt instruments, in the words of one interoffice memorandum, were to be "U.S. Government bonds with the principal linked to some price index (either U.S. or foreign) which are specially issued to a particular purchaser and are not offered generally to the public."[16] When the Treasury's general counsel determined that such an offering would be illegal, the idea was dropped. According to a briefing paper prepared for a Treasury official about to go before a congressional subcommittee, the idea was dropped because "the U.S. position regarding foreign investment is to support the free flow of cap-

---

[16] Reprinted in U.S. Congress, House, Committee on Government Operations, *Federal Response to OPEC*, part 1, pp. 472–73. The memorandum was dated April 1976.

FIGURE 5.1. The add-on agreement.

ḷꞏꞏꞏ ꞏ   1975

MEMORANDUM TO THE SECRETARY OF STATE

Subject: Special Arrangements for Purchase of U.S.
           Government Securities by the Saudi Arabian
           Government

SUMMARY

        In recent months we have had extensive discussions
with officials of the Saudi Arabian Monetary Agency (SAMA)
concerning investments in U.S. Government Securities. In
December we reached an understanding whereby SAMA will
purchase new issues of marketable U.S. Treasury obligations
with a maturity of one year or more through a special
arrangement involving the Federal Reserve Bank of New York,
as agent. Purchases under this arrangement over the next
six months are expected to be approximately $2.5 billion.
This amount will be in addition to any other acquisitions
of Treasury or United States agency obligations made by the
Saudis through other channels or at shorter maturities.
It should be emphasized that this arrangement does not
involve issues specially designed for the Saudis, but
rather constitutes special purchases of marketable securities

THE ARRANGEMENT

        In December, 1974, in Jidda, the Treasury reached
agreement with SAMA to establish a new relationship through
the Federal Reserve Bank of New York with the Treasury
borrowing operation. Under this arrangement SAMA will
purchase new U.S. Treasury securities with maturities of at
least one year. When announcement of a Treasury offering is
made, the Federal Reserve will query SAMA immediately as to
its interest in purchasing additional amounts of the same
issue at the average price of the auction. Should SAMA
desire to acquire any such securities, it will inform the
Federal Reserve Bank of its interest prior to the auction.
The mechanics of payment, deposit of securities, etc., will
be handled between SAMA and the Federal Reserve.   Should SAMA
wish to sell these securities prior to maturity, it will
offer Treasury for two days the opportunity to repurchase the
securities at the then prevailing market price. While the
current arrangement is limited to new marketable securities,

With the removal of the
deleted part of this document,
this document is unclassified.   ﺳﺮّي ﻟﻠﻐﺎﻳﺔ

SOURCE: Reprinted in U.S. Congress, House, Committee on Government Operations, *Federal Response to OPEC*, part 1, pp. 467–68 (*continued*).

---

ital across international boundaries. Furthermore, if this flow is to work
to the maximum benefit of all countries, it must remain, as far as possible, *undistorted by artificial impediments and incentives.*" The paper went
on to claim that U.S. recycling policies were based on the premise that
free markets were the most efficient means of allocating international
capital flows. The author also pointed out that the United States had

FIGURE 5.1. *Continued.*

in the future SAMA may request that we consider issuing on
a similar basis an additional issue of securities of a type
already outstanding and non-marketable securities of a
short-term duration specially tailored to fit a short-term
investment need of SAMA.

The principal advantage to the Saudis of this arrangement is that it will avoid the disruption to the market
occasioned by large security purchases or sales on their
part. It should be emphasized that the purchases are at the
auction average. Thus we are giving the Saudis no interest
rate advantage compared with other lenders.

The amount of special purchases contemplated is approximately ███████████ over the next six months. We expect the
Saudis to continue in addition to purchase short-term
Treasury securities through normal market procedures as well
as to purchase securities of sponsored U.S. agencies such as
the Federal National Mortgage Association. At present outstanding Saudi holdings of U.S. Government Securities is
██████████ of which ██████ is in the form of notes
purchased under the special arrangement. Another ██████
of notes under the special arrangement have been purchased
for delivery on February 18.

The sine-qua-non for the Saudis in this arrangement is
confidentiality and we have assured them that we will do
everything in our power to comply with their desires.

/S/ *Jack F. Bennett*
Jack F. Bennett

With the removal of the deleted
part of this document, this document
is unclassified.

"continually stated in the OECD that we would take no special discriminatory action that would attract OPEC funds to the U.S."[17]

In fact, the "specials" were not offered to SAMA because the Treasury
could not legally do so. In the memo reprinted in Figure 5.1 it is clearly
stated that the Treasury wanted to offer nonmarketable securities. Special incentives to the Saudis were offered in the add-on arrangement,
and Treasury officials' testimony to Congress must be seen as public justifications. The add-on arrangement was a "special discriminatory action" that attracted OPEC funds to the United States.

Proof that the agreement had worked was not long in coming. Just
weeks after the trip, an official in the New York Fed's Foreign Department reported that he was "now managing a very substantial petrodollar
portfolio," of which only $1,000 was in cash. Almost all of this money
had come in the preceding weeks from two Arab countries. One was
Saudi Arabia, and the other most likely the United Arab Emirates (primarily from Abu Dhabi).[18] By the fourth quarter of 1977, Saudi Arabia
accounted for twenty percent of all holdings of Treasury notes and

[17] Schotta to Bosworth.
[18] Willett to Bennett.

bonds by foreign central banks. From the time of the add-on arrangement to the last quarter of 1977, the proportion of U.S. investments by Middle Eastern oil exporters in Treasury bonds and notes rose from 43 percent to 65 percent. Of the Treasury obligations held by those Middle Eastern countries, Saudi Arabia held 90 percent. This was an accomplishment, Anthony M. Solomon (then under secretary of the treasury for international monetary affairs) testified. The investments were much less liquid than the bank deposits in which Middle East oil exporters had kept 90 percent of their U.S. investments in 1974.[19]

In addition to the add-on arrangement, officials from the Department of Commerce traveled to Saudi Arabia to market Federal National Mortgage Association (FNMA, popularly "Fannie Mae") securities. In December 1975, an internal study at the Fed concluded:

> To the extent that U.S. banks limit their accepting of short-term deposits from OPEC members as a result of policy suasion, and to the extent that OPEC members may not easily evade banks' attempts to limit such deposits, some tendency may delop for OPEC members to redistribute their U.S. assets over a wider range, by type and maturity, of instruments. . . .
>
> A shift of OPEC members' funds into mortgages might promote a current Federal Reserve goal.[20]

There is no hard evidence that the Fed implemented its plan to limit OPEC's short-term deposits by "unofficial Federal Reserve discussion with those banks holding the largest deposits," and U.S. bankers are loath to talk about cooperating with government authorities.[21] It is likely more than coincidence, however, that Saudi capital soon shifted from call deposits at banks to government-backed mortgage funds.

Table 3.2 shows that compared with the Kuwaiti monetary authorities, whom U.S. officials felt they were *not* successful in influencing, SAMA has much more of its portfolio in dollars, in the United States, and in U.S. government debt. In fact, at one point in 1978, 70 percent of all Saudi assets in the United States were held in an account by the New York Federal Reserve Bank. Only 5 percent of Kuwaiti reserves are in Treasury issues, and none are held by the New York Fed. It is possible that a large portfolio might put its reserves into U.S. Treasury instru-

[19] Miller, "U.S. Securities Draw More OPEC Dollars," *New York Times*, p. A1; testimony of Anthony M. Solomon, U.S. Congress, Senate, Committee on Foreign Relations, *Witteveen Facility and the OPEC Financial Surpluses.*

[20] Adams and Fleisig, "Reduction of Short-Term Capital Inflows."

[21] Interview with Arthur Scully, Morgan Guaranty Bank, New York City, September 1983.

ments without any prompting. The counterargument is that Kuwait, act-ing on purely economic grounds, put almost no money into Treasuries. There are, of course, reasons for the differences between the two coun-tries' portfolios that are explicable by financial strategies.[22] These differ-ing reasons do not, however, account for the fact that Saudi purchases are from central bank to central bank, while Kuwaiti purchases are made privately.

In the 1970s SAMA investments were made by eight investment advis-ers—four from White Weld (later owned by Merrill Lynch) and four from Baring Brothers. Each month they were given an estimate of what SAMA had to invest abroad in the coming four weeks. The investment advisers submitted an investment plan to their Saudi superiors for ap-proval. According to three advisers in the 1980s, they were not given in-structions on what financial instruments they were to use. After receiv-ing a monthly plan, however, the deputy governor of SAMA might hypothetically ask them to write a report outlining what effects greater purchases of T-bills would have on the overall performance and struc-ture of the portfolio.[23]

Investment decisions at SAMA were subject to three criteria: price, secrecy, and avoidance of moving the market. Therefore, "on average, over a period of time, the add-on arrangement is advantageous" to SAMA.[24] In 1974, recalled the U.S. political secretary in Riyadh, Minis-ter of Finance Abalkhail was the only financial expert in Saudi Arabia. "His attitude was better safe than sorry," and that favored the most conservative investment available, which was Treasury securities.[25] David Mulford, the first adviser to SAMA from White Weld, was said to be "the architect of the SAMA portfolio."[26] Mulford claimed that there was absolutely nothing political about SAMA investments.[27] Less than one year after that interview he became assistant secretary for interna-tional affairs in the Department of the Treasury. One of his first acts in office was to propose that the Treasury issue general bearer bonds to increase the confidentiality of foreign holders of U.S. government debt.

If we assume that Mulford's claims are not credible, then we can

[22] An excellent study that details the different financial strategies is Mattione, *OPEC's In-vestments.*

[23] Interviews with three investment advisers to SAMA, Riyadh, November 1984.

[24] Ibid.

[25] Interview with David Patterson, political secretary, U.S. Embassy, Riyadh, 29 October 1984.

[26] Interview with John Ives, U.S. Treasury attaché, Riyadh, 30 October 1984.

[27] Interview with David Mulford, Princeton, New Jersey, 1983.

begin to piece together minimal and maximal explanations of how U.S. influence worked. The minimal explanation is that Saudi officials were attracted to the incentives offered by the U.S. Treasury. Although secrecy per se is an unusual financial criterion for an investment strategy, SAMA investors purchased Treasury issues for what they perceived to be economically rational reasons. By this interpretation, U.S. influence was achieved by virtue of its ability to give market incentives to an international investor.

There is evidence that U.S. influence was more explicit. For one, businessmen are among the many who sometimes like to aggrandize their roles in the course of events, and the investment advisers working for SAMA are no exception. Though they claim to be making all of the day-to-day investment decisions, there is at least one example of a major purchase of U.S. government obligations that had no input from SAMA's foreign advisers. In 1974, an American investment banker met with executives of the FNMA. He advised them of opportunities to sell securities to SAMA, and shortly afterward Oakley Hunter and Robert Bennett of FNMA met with Anwar Ali, governor of SAMA. During 1974 FNMA made two or three placements with SAMA, the total value of which was approximately $1 billion. The placements were handled by the New York Fed after they had been approved by the Treasury Department.[28] There is no evidence that investment advisers to SAMA were consulted about the $1 billion investment, though they were supposedly responsible for such activity. Only four years later, by which time Treasury officials had asked FNMA to let them handle placing the securities of all government agencies, did David Mulford visit FNMA offices in Washington, D.C.[29]

If it is possible that one billion U.S. dollars were invested in the securities of a government agency without consulting with "the architect of SAMA's portfolio," it is also possible that SAMA purchased Treasury securities without the knowledge of investment advisers who deny a political bias to their employer's financial strategies. It is, therefore, quite possible that SAMA and Saudi Ministry of Finance officials were not only responding to market incentives but to direct U.S. pressure.

In short, we may be sure of a minimalist explanation of Saudi acqui-

---

[28] Interview with Michael Palmer, New York, 21 and 23 September 1983.

[29] The visit occurred on 29 August 1978. See U.S. Congress, House, Committee on Government Operations, *Operations of Federal Agencies*, part 2, p. 359. Bennet testified under oath that he never directly made deals with SAMA, though he met with SAMA officials more than twenty-two times. The banker present at the meetings in 1974 remembers differently.

escence to T-bill purchases and have good reason to expect a less equivocal explanation. At the very least, SAMA placed a substantial portion of its portfolio in U.S. government obligations because American statespeople were able to alter the market so as to give Saudi Arabia a greater incentive to do so. Quite possibly, the line of influence was more direct and less subtle. A former American ambassador to the Middle East attributes Saudi purchases of T-bills to an explicit U.S. offer "to provide a security umbrella for the Gulf."[30] If this is so, the success of the United States in recruiting SAMA funds is easier to understand and theoretically more interesting to the political economist. Unfortunately, such an agreement would have to be secret and informal (or else it would be subject to confirmation by the Congress), and therefore evidence of it is difficult to find.

CONTINUITY OF UNILATERALISM

Much of the U.S. reaction to the problem of recycling came at the nadir in global perceptions of its power. The administration that followed was much more bent toward multilateral institutions and cooperation. If the exploitative nature of American handling of the petrodollar transfer problem was caused by a particular administration, then the case for functional regimes in the future may be more optimistic than presented in this book. A systemic-level analysis of petrodollar recycling should hold true, no matter what administration is in power. If one administration is more multilateralist than another, and outcomes are more cooperative, then the efficacy of an analysis based on international relations is reduced.

Petrodollar recycling took place during both Republican and Democratic administrations. The Carter administration had stated goals of becoming more multilateralist. The outcomes that followed those policies, however, I have argued, continued the trend of American delegitimation. While the policy goals were putatively bound by the normative constraints of legitimate hegemony, Carter administration officials pursued policies that produced the same outcomes as their predecessors. Delegitimation of American hegemony not only continued but became a new equilibrium of agency.

Foreign policy makers in the Carter administration were deeply influ-

[30] Interview, Boston, December 1985.

enced by the conclusions of the Trilateral Commission and thus were nominally more oriented toward multilateral cooperation than their predecessors. While the Trilateral Commission advocated an approach to OPEC that was less confrontational than that of Kissinger, it agreed with the concept of a financial safety net and indeed put even greater emphasis on it. Its Task Force Report on OPEC called for recycling arrangements through the OECD.[31] In general, the Trilateral Commission had called for greater policy coordination among industrialized nations. Its reports predicted that cooperation could be achieved through coordination.

As under secretary of state for economic affairs, Richard N. Cooper was the perfect candidate to make America's approach to recycling more cooperative. He was the author of a seminal work on economic interdependence in 1968, long before that subject drew the attention of other scholars. He also held a personal and intellectual belief that Prisoners' Dilemmas in the international political economy can be overcome by policy coordination.[32]

Many other officials went to Washington in 1977 who were multilateralist or members of the Trilateral Commission (and frequently both). Both the Departments of State and the Treasury were occupied by people who had learned the gospel of policy coordination from the Trilateral Commission. These men and women were intellectually committed to the idea of cooperation in the international political economy, and many remain believers to the present day. Joseph Nye, a formative influence on liberal theories of international relations, worked with the International Energy Agency. Michael Blumenthal, though not an academic, continues to write thoughtful articles on the importance of interdependence in a world increasingly brought together by information flows and commercial intercourse.[33]

Yet these influential and thoughtful policy makers did not markedly diverge from the paths defined in less multilateralist administrations. Cooper recalls that by 1978 the Treasury was no longer interested in recruiting Saudi funds because by then it seemed to him that markets were working to recycle the Arab surplus. He did pursue legislation for the Safety Net in Congress because the former administration had made an international commitment to do so, but this effort was abandoned when it became clear that there would never be enough votes to

---

[31] Trilateral Commission, *Task Force Reports*, p. 157.
[32] Cooper, *Economics of Interdependence.*
[33] Blumenthal, "World Economy and Technological Change."

pass the Financial Support Fund Act. Cooper continued the previous policies of the Nixon and Ford administrations for petrodollar recycling because "I am a strong believer in continuity of foreign policy across administrations."[34]

These recollections are consistent with other statements made by officials of the U.S. government (from the Treasury, Fed, and Commerce) to congressional committees and in public statements. Yet internal memorandums from that period suggest that the Treasury was very concerned with maintaining Saudi investment in U.S. markets (in general, and in government securities). Rather than following its multilateral rhetoric, the Carter administration continued to compete for Saudi funds.

The biggest issue in 1978 was that of withholding figures on investment from the numerous members of Congress who had requested them. By August 1978, the Department of the Treasury had received requests from different committees and subcommittees of the House of Representatives and the Senate, including the Church Committee on Multinational Corporations, the Scheuer Committee, and the Rosenthal Committee.[35] Not only did the Treasury scramble to ensure that legal opinion would preclude disclosure, but it also attempted to prevent the flow of information from any other government body, and it reassured the Saudis that information would never be disclosed.

In preparation of talking points for Treasury Secretary Blumenthal's 1978 meeting with the Saudi minister of finance, two members of the joint commission made the following observations:

> We believe that we will be able to maintain the confidentiality of the detail Saudi Arabian investment data which we hold but given current pressures, there is some risk that we will not be successful. Perhaps the Saudis should be told of current developments concerning this issue.
>
> In your discussions with Saudi Arabian officials you may wish to draw on the following talking points:
> —In recent months we have received a number of requests from Con-

---

[34] Interview with Richard N. Cooper, Cambridge, Mass., 8 July 1987.

[35] The Church Committee was formally titled the Subcommittee on Multinational Corporations of the Committee on Foreign Relations of the United States Senate. Hearings held from late January through March 1975 were titled "The Political and Financial Consequences of the OPEC Price Increase." The Rosenthal Committee was formally a subcommittee of the Committee on Government Operations of the House of Representatives. Most of the hearings focused on OPEC financial flows and took place from 1978 to 1981. The General Accounting Office also made several requests for investment data, most of which were in September 1979.

gress, the press, and private citizens for information on the investments of
your country in the U.S.

—We have resisted the disclosure of this information to all requestors
on both legal and policy grounds. To date, we have been successful in these
efforts.

—A basic principle of this administration's policy on inward foreign investment is to accord privacy to individual investor's decisions.

—We appreciate your continued use of U.S. capital markets and will continue to the maximum extent possible to keep the details of your assets in
the U.S. confidential.[36]

If markets were working efficiently to recycle petrodollars, the obvious question is why the Treasury was so concerned with enforcing an
agreement made in secret in 1974 to keep Saudi holdings secret, and
why Secretary Blumenthal was supposed to express U.S. appreciation
for Saudi placements in U.S. markets. To credit Cooper's argument,
however, it seems equally obvious that Treasury efforts to prevent disclosure were aimed not simply at Saudi investment in Treasury obligations, or even at Saudi investments in the United States, but rather at
Saudi dollar holdings in general.

The effort to which the Treasury went to avoid offending Saudi Arabia is exemplified in a series of Treasury memorandums and letters in
late 1978—a set of writings that is the most amusing body of correspondence between bureaucrats that I have ever seen. It started with a
five-paragraph report on the Dow Jones wire on 13 September 1978,
reporting a Soviet move out of the dollar and into the Deutsche mark,
but discounting the effects of such a move on the dollar's global position.[37] The report cited "intelligence sources" for the information. This
was very upsetting to F. Lisle Widman because if the CIA disclosed Soviet investments outside of the United States, he thought, then the
Saudis might get nervous about the confidentiality of their investments. Therefore, Blumenthal should warn CIA director Stansfield
Turner not to release figures on Soviet holdings so as not to jeopardize
continued Saudi investments. "Frankly, I am worried," he wrote, "about
the continued circulation by the CIA in its classified, but widely circu-
lated, documents of detailed statistics on dollar holdings of individual
countries." (Saudi Arabia is only the Arab member of OPEC for which
such figures are classified state secrets.) "You will recall that the CIA

[36] Palmer and Munk to Blumenthal.
[37] "U.S. Officials Discount Reports Soviets Dumping Dollars in Forex [Foreign Ex-
change] Markets," Washington 2"16G, 13 SEF 78.

prepared a table for the State Department offering quite precise details on Saudi Arabian dollar holdings," Widman also wrote, and "it was only our intervention which prevented that from being transmitted to Congress."[38] The irony of a Treasury official suggesting that the CIA was not secretive enough about Soviet dollar holdings was amplified in a memorandum from the "National Security" assistant to the secretary of the treasury.[39] He pointed out to Widman that the CIA had given the Dow Jones reporter published figures from the Bank for International Settlements—figures that are available to anybody. Still, just two months later, Blumenthal wrote to the United States director of intelligence Admiral Stansfield Turner ("Dear Stan"), warning him in essence that loose lips sink ships. "Should information on these [Middle East Oil Exporters'] holdings be divulged . . . I am afraid that this could precipitate a significant reversal in the investment policies of these governments, both with regard to their holdings in the U.S. and in dollars."[40] Turner replied, "None of the individuals involved (in giving the information to Dow Jones) had access to Treasury information on foreign assets; in fact, they were not even aware that Treasury provided the Agency with such information." Turner also reminded the treasury secretary that he was instructed by law to provide Congress and other agencies of the government (e.g., the State Department) with intelligence. The information on OPEC assets was, however, never disclosed.[41]

If further indication of the Treasury Department's concern for protecting Saudi confidentiality need be provided, it comes in a memo prepared (but apparently never sent) by the Bureau of Economic Analysis (BEA) in the Department of Commerce. Citing the refusal of the Treasury to release to the BEA information about capital flows from Saudi Arabia, Kuwait, Iran, and Bahrain, the memo complains: "This lack of country detail hinders the work of the Balance of Payments Division in compiling . . . the international transaction accounts and investment position of the United States."[42] It was thus the position of the Department of the Treasury that ensuring the continued flow of Arab capital into U.S. markets was more important than attempts by the Department of

[38] Widman to Solomon.

[39] Collins to Solomon.

[40] Blumenthal to Turner.

[41] Turner to Blumenthal. Four lines of the letter, apparently describing the types of reports that make reference to Treasury figures, were deleted prior to declassification.

[42] Commerce Department Memorandum, "Request for individual country data from Treasury International Capital reporting on oil-exporting countries" (to and from are blank), 28 November 1978, "Draft" on BEA stationery.

Commerce to calculate the investment position of the United States in the global economy.

Though it was less concerned with the secrecy of Arab investments, the CIA concurred that OPEC money continued to have a great potential for disrupting markets if an Arab government became displeased with U.S. policy: "Temporary dislocation of international financial markets would ensue, if the Saudi Arabian government ever chose to use its accumulated wealth as a political weapon."[43] The report went on to note that Saudi reserves were greater than those of the United States and West Germany combined.

Secrecy would not have been important to officials of the Carter administration unless they continued to recruit unilaterally an abnormally large share of Saudi wealth. In the summer of 1979, officials of the State Department were warned by high Saudi officials that if the United States made public OPEC investment data, they would transfer their funds to other countries.[44] The CIA, while anticipating a major financial problem if the Saudis used their money as a political weapon, did not see a problem with being more lax about releasing figures to Congress.

OIL PRICES AND DOLLARS

So long as OPEC oil was priced in U.S. dollars, and so long as OPEC invested the dollars in U.S. government instruments, the U.S. government enjoyed a double loan. The first part of the loan was for oil. The government could print dollars to pay for oil, and the American economy did not have to produce goods and services in exchange for the oil until OPEC used the dollars for goods and services. Obviously, the strategy could not work if dollars were not a means of exchange for oil.

The second part of the loan was from all other economies that had to pay dollars for oil but could not print currency. Those economies had to trade their goods and services for dollars in order to pay OPEC. Again, so long as OPEC held the dollars rather than spending them, the United States received a loan. It was, therefore, important to keep

[43] CIA, "Saudi Arabian Foreign Investment." The mimeo is marked "Secret, Not Releasable to Foreign Nationals" and was reviewed for declassification in May 1985. It has no other markings to indicate who wrote it for whom.

[44] Two memos have been published in a declassified form, which do not mention the country involved or the specific branch of the U.S. government from which the memo came. This additional information was told to the author in not-for-attribution interviews, Washington, D.C., August 1983. See U.S. Congress, House, Committee on Government Operations, *Federal Response to OPEC*, part 1, pp. 446–47.

OPEC oil priced in dollars at the same time that government officials continued to recruit Arab funds.

OPEC, however, began to perceive the advantages of pegging the price of oil to a basket of currencies, especially as the dollar depreciated after Jimmy Carter took office. In June 1975, OPEC had reached a consensus on pegging the price of oil to SDRs (Standard Drawing Rights in the IMF), but the dollar began to appreciate shortly afterward, and the decision was forgotten.[45] OPEC discussions on pegging the price of oil to different currencies were never made public, but they were apparently made known to the U.S. Department of the Treasury. A memo on talking points for use by a Treasury official in Saudi Arabia lists three options that OPEC had discussed.[46] One was called the "Geneva II basket," which would have been composed of the Group of Ten countries (i.e., BIS members) plus Switzerland and Austria. A second option was "a strong currency basket," which seems to have meant that they would link the price of oil to whatever currency was appreciating. A link to SDRs was the third option and the one that was considered most seriously.

From December 1977 to September 1978, the relative purchasing power parity of OPEC dollar-denominated assets fell by a total of 40 percent.[47] This meant that when OPEC's imports in all currencies were weighted to reflect the changes in the exchange rates of the goods they were paying for, the dollars they were paid for oil bought 40 percent less than in November 1977. In effect, OPEC had lowered the price of oil—though not on purpose—by four-tenths. Its investments, to the extent that they were in dollars, were also hurt. In the estimation of the Treasury Department, Saudi Arabia would have been better off using a basket of currencies to price oil for all but eighteen months of the period since early 1973.

The Saudis, however, had the greatest proportion of dollar-denominated reserves in OPEC. This meant that their reserves were diminished by the depreciation of the dollar (compared to the basket of their imports). But it also meant that they had the most to lose if a shift by OPEC to a basket of currencies threatened international confidence in the dollar. Having agreed to invest so much in dollars, the Saudis now

[45] U.S. Congress, House, Committee on Banking, Finance, and Urban Affairs, *OPEC's Proposal to Peg the Price of Oil.*

[46] U.S. Treasury Department, "The Dollar and the Pricing Unit for Oil," mimeo, 26 October 1978.

[47] U.S. Treasury Department, "Movements in the Relative Purchasing Power of OPEC Dollar Denominated Assets," mimeo, 23 October 1978.

shared a stake in maintaining the dollar as an international reserve currency. On the one hand, dollars constituted 90 percent of Saudi government revenues in 1979, and those revenues were subject to the same fluctuations as the dollar. On the other hand, Saudi investments were, at roughly the same time, 83 percent dollar denominated.[48] The choice was whether to stabilize current revenues while threatening the worth of all past revenues (since invested in dollar assets).

U.S. officials responded to threatening rumbles in OPEC meetings and, more important, to the diversification of investments by holders of large OPEC surpluses. In late 1978 SAMA began what the CIA called "a modest diversification program, converting small amounts of dollars into other currencies."[49] Two investment managers in SAMA recalled that the program was more than modest. SAMA, according to them, was preparing to engage in a massive shift to Deutsche marks and yen.[50] Kuwait, which had always diversified its reserves, intensified the shift from the dollar.

At the same time the dollar continued its slide downward, the sale of advanced fighter aircraft to Saudi Arabia became an issue in Congress. On 7 March 1978, Kuwaiti minister of finance Atiqi visited Saudi Arabia, and (according to a Treasury Department briefing paper) he suggested not only a move to a basket but a price hike as well. The position of the Treasury Department was that "confidence in the dollar remains fragile. Recent and more frequent news reports regarding OPEC's growing disenchantment with use of [the] dollar for oil pricing further disturb the market. If OPEC changed the unit of accounting for oil pricing it could precipitate a major market reaction which would be in the interest neither of the Saudis, other OPEC members, nor the U.S."[51]

The briefing paper also noted that Secretary of State Cyrus Vance had recently noted the importance of U.S.-Saudi cooperation and recommended that the U.S.-Saudi joint economic commission produce projects for Saudi Arabia "with highly visible, tangible results." Treasury had therefore agreed to disburse $500,000 for a solar energy project, but it concluded that "there is little the commission can do to offset pos-

---

[48] U.S. Treasury Department, "Saudi Exchange Rate Policy," mimeo. The paper bears markings indicating it was declassified by Russel Munk on 10 September 1979.

[49] Office of International Banking and Portfolio Investment, no title, mimeo, 21 November 1978. This memo was drafted and reviewed by men who are listed on other documents as Treasury officials, but the memo was classified by the CIA, citing "sensitive intelligence sources and methods involved," and was never declassified. It is therefore unclear what agency in the executive branch it was written for.

[50] Interviews with three investment advisers to SAMA, Riyadh, November 1984.

[51] Bergsten to Blumenthal, pp. 1–2.

sible Saudi disappointment over lack of a peace settlement in the Middle East or failure to sell them F-15 fighter aircraft."[52]

The talking points that Treasury formulated for Blumenthal's annual meeting with the Saudi finance minister focused on convincing him that the dollar would soon appreciate. Blumenthal's briefing book for the meeting suggested that he emphasize the president's commitment to a strong dollar and to reducing the budget deficit. As part of the program to achieve a strong dollar, the book notes that "the President understands that . . . easing of interest rates can occur only when there are signs that the effort to curb inflation is succeeding."[53]

The bulk of the talking points, however, are an argument on the merits of the dollar as compared to the SDR. While one point subtly pointed out that harm to the dollar would wipe out Saudi reserves, and the words "common interest" are not rare in the briefing, the thrust of Blumenthal's discussion with Abalkhail apparently centered on the IMF.[54]

Indeed, by the autumn of 1978, the Saudis had made it clear to U.S. officials that they would view increased power at the IMF in a very favorable light. As part of a complicated deal, (see the beginning of this chapter) the United States found itself agreeing reluctantly to Saudi participation in the IMF in return for Saudi agreement not to allow the SDR to become a meaningful reserve currency.

The outcome is obvious. Oil is still priced in dollars, and the SDR has never gained much recognition as a replacement for the dollar in international reserves. This is a double representation of American unilateralism during the Carter years. Treasury officials worked very hard to keep oil priced in dollars. They also managed to keep tight rein on the extent to which cooperative regimes such as the IMF could assume responsibility for petrodollar recycling.

Legitimate principles of hegemonic rule, as defined by policy makers, were hardly what an ethical philosopher would prescribe. They validated the allocation of goods and capital by free markets, except when market forces represented a shift in the distribution of capabilities away

---

[52] Ibid.

[53] U.S. Treasury Department, "The Dollar and the Pricing of Oil," a section from a briefing book prepared for Blumenthal's meeting with Saudi finance minister Abalkhail in October 1978. The quote is from the first page of the section.

[54] Shortly after his meeting with Abalkhail, Blumenthal began to talk down the dollar, and the Bundesbank ended its support for the dollar. This policy not only contradicted Blumenthal's intimations to the Saudis about support for a strong dollar but also seemed to fly in the face of the macroeconomic policy coordination agreed to at the Bonn Summit. See Oye, *Economic Discrimination and Political Exchange*, esp. pp. 179–84.

from the United States and from the industrialized world. Political intervention in international markets was to be allowed, indeed called for, but only if it was on a multilateral basis, and not to the exclusive benefit of one country. Market forces were thus an ex post facto legitimation of America's endeavor to reassert its hegemonic dominance. This endeavor was bounded only by the constraints of multilateral coordination.

Yet even these minimal constraints were routinely ignored by U.S. policy makers, who were clearly cognizant of them. While promising to avoid competitive trade policies, the United States instituted the Joint Commission for Economic Cooperation with Saudi Arabia that earned more than $500 million in deposits for feasibility studies alone. While promising not to offer OPEC nations special incentives to attract their capital, the United States agreed to an add-on arrangement, which allowed SAMA to purchase Treasury bonds outside of the competitive auctions in which every other state had to participate.[55] Though it was expected that SAMA would turn to U.S. capital markets to dispose of its surplus, and this was not illegitimate on the part of the United States, it was clearly something more than the laws of supply and demand that resulted in 70 percent of all Saudi assets in the United States being held in a New York Fed account.

Not only were U.S. actions illegitimate; they actively discouraged international policy coordination. The agreements that were concluded (though never put into effect) were to the advantage of the United States, and when they were not (as in the IMF oil facility) the United States made cooperation more difficult. The United States attempted to regain *temps perdu*. It sought to reestablish the period during which the equilibrium of international market forces produced favorable outcomes and during which its dominance was not questioned. Yet in seeking to regain this equilibrium, by virtue of its deviation from the precepts of its hegemonic rule, the United States moved the world to a new equilibrium of exploitation.

During the Carter administration, officials responsible for foreign economic policy were more multilateralist than their predecessors, but their policies continued to demonstrate unilateralism and a widening divergence from the norms of legitimate hegemony. Though they professed to believe in the utility of those norms more than the officials of

---

[55] When word of the add-on arrangement leaked out, it was offered to other central banks in both OPEC and the industrialized world. Today it is used principally by Japan. See U.S. General Accounting Office, *Are OPEC Financial Holdings a Danger to U.S. Banks or the Economy?*, pp. 10–11.

previous administrations, their actions were equally illegitimate, if not more so.

In an attempt to continue the recruitment of Saudi funds, and in competition with other industrial powers, the State and Treasury Departments went to extraordinary lengths to prevent the Congress from gathering information. The secretary of the treasury even went to the trouble of making sure the CIA remained secretive. It was this secrecy, not accorded the investments of any other nations, that led the Commerce Department to complain that it was unable to compile accurate data on either foreign investment in the United States or its balance-of-payments.

CHAPTER SIX

The Interpretation of Hegemony

This concluding chapter reviews the three competing explanations and explores generalizations that might be made based on those findings. First, I review what happened in international capital markets and what it means to say that "markets worked." Then I ask whether petrodollars really were recycled, or whether we live in a world that is more anarchic than even realists claim. I next discuss how this case infirms and confirms liberal institutionalism and hegemonic stability theory. In the conclusion, I argue for a new method of interpreting international political economy, based on the intersubjective framework in which power and markets are constructed.

DID "MARKETS WORK"?

In theory, markets work when goods are distributed on the basis of the price mechanism. Market forces are the summation of individual actions, none of which is intended to bring about a market, but all of which result in higher utilities for individuals. In practice, such a theory is difficult (if not impossible) to test when examining government debts. When we review why observers claim that markets worked to recycle petrodollars, we see that what they actually mean in practice is quite different from the theory. This section reviews the various uses of the term *market forces*. Saying that markets worked ranges in meaning:

- *the location of funds*—if funds were placed in markets, then markets must have worked.

- *intermediation*—banks channeled funds from savers to borrowers.
- *politically motivated speech*—saying that markets were working calmed fears that otherwise might have led to market failure.
- *power outcome*—the imposition of market forces on a situation where legitimate principles called for non-market-based allocation.
- *automaticity*—markets function automatically, so whatever happened was by definition market forces.

Location versus Agency

In its simplest form, the conventional wisdom on petrodollar recycling asserts that oil exporters invested their capital surpluses in international banking markets, and banks then lent the money to oil importers with trade deficits. This simplistic notion of recycling is most certainly incorrect.

Saudi Arabia accumulated more than $200 billion from 1973 to 1982, which was 50 percent of the OPEC surplus; and Kuwait and the United Arab Emirates accounted for another 25 percent of the total.[1] Saudi Arabia placed approximately 45 percent of its capital in banks, but it also placed 30 percent in the hands of the U.S. government. Twenty-four percent of the total OPEC surplus was placed in the Eurobanking market (which includes offshore branches of U.S. banks), and 22 percent of the total was placed in the United States (and about half of that was in government obligations).[2] Other developed nations received $118 billion (30 percent), LDCs got 19 percent, mostly in the form of aid, and international financial institutions received 5 percent.

While Saudi investment in U.S. government obligations involved conscious policies and decisions, the bulk of funds that ended up in capital markets seems to have been placed there almost by default. Unable to handle such large deposits, many banks offered negative real interest rates on OPEC deposits immediately after the first oil shock.

As I argued in Chapter 3, the intermediate destination of petrodollar flows gives only half of the picture of recycling. It is also important to examine the sources of financing in nations with oil-related trade deficits. Two groups of nations had deficits: other developed countries (i.e., the

---

[1] Ecuador, Indonesia, Nigeria, and Algeria compiled current account deficits of $30 billion, which means that Saudi Arabia, Kuwait, and the United Arab Emirates actually held 82 percent of the OPEC current account surplus. Iran ended up with 9 percent of the surplus, while Libya, Iraq, and Qatar split the rest.

[2] Mattione, *OPEC's Investments*, pp. 12–14. The amount he could not account for probably includes $12 billion in Swiss banks and some underestimation of gold purchases.

advanced industrialized democracies besides the five largest economies) and LDCs. The developed nations were able to turn to international capital markets for financing, and they deposited more funds in Eurobanks than they borrowed. There was, therefore, no need for petrodollar recycling to developed nations. The OPEC funds that they received were in excess of their financing needs, and those needs were provided for by the capital surpluses of the Big Five developed economies.

LDCs, in contrast, had very little access to Eurobanking markets, contrary to the conventional wisdom. A small number of newly industrialized countries borrowed the bulk of funds available to LDCs, and these funds were not directly related to oil imports but rather to purchases of factories and machinery from developed nations. Aside from the small group of indebted NICs, LDCs either received capital from official sources (governments and international financial institutions) or they were forced to import less.

As the analysis in Chapter 3 showed, there was an inverse correlation between increased sovereign borrowing and increased oil imports (both as a proportion of GNP). Capital markets were most likely to lend to nations that did not suffer from the oil shocks. The small number of LDCs that borrowed most between 1973 and 1981 were NICs and oil exporters. To the extent that a nation's external oil trade played a part in determining whether it would receive new funds from commercial banks, new lending flowed to oil exporters. Banks, in effect, recycled funds from oil exporters with a capital surplus to oil exporters with trade deficits. Intermediation did not occur between oil exporters and importers.

This makes intuitive sense because we expect capital markets to allocate funds based on risk and rates of return, not on normative or political criteria. Loan officers were loath to lend to LDCs with high oil bills because they were less likely than NICs and oil exporters to run the trade surpluses requisite for repayment of the loans. No economist would predict that capital markets would fund countries that are poor credit risks.[3]

Indeed, Benjamin Cohen argued fairly early on that there was a potential mismatch between oil-exporting nations with a surplus and oil-importing nations with a deficit. He pointed out that financial flows

---

[3] By 1989 it was clear to at least some officials that the "conventional wisdom" on recycling was incorrect. The staff director of the Division of International Finance at the Fed Board of Governors wrote: "The proportion of the OPEC surplus that was actually recycled through the banking system was very small" (Truman, "U.S. Policy," p. 728).

might go to NICs to pay for industrialization.[4] Yet even this more nuanced description attributes the distribution of surpluses and deficits to factors that are exogenous to financial markets.

To argue that markets were intermediaries is to take as given the distribution of surpluses and deficits. The process of intermediation is not supposed to determine who has the deficits. But a nation usually could not run a trade deficit unless it was financed with foreign capital. Financing, in fact, determined who ran a deficit rather than the converse.[5]

Intermediation

In 1978, half of all publicly guaranteed debt from commercial banks to LDCs was held by Brazil (20 percent), Mexico (18 percent), Algeria (9 percent), and Venezuela (5 percent). Brazil presumably was able to borrow on the basis of exports, while Mexico, Algeria, and Venezuela were major oil producers. The next largest ten LDC borrowers held another 27 percent of the total sovereign debt. Only 21 percent of the flow of private credit guaranteed by governments went to the remaining seventy-one LDCs in the world.

Political stability and international patronage also played a role in how banks made lending decisions. Senegal, for example, borrowed $438 million in government-guaranteed debt from private creditors from 1970 to 1980.[6] Devastated by drought in addition to higher energy prices, Senegal did not have much to promise by way of export earnings (its primary export is groundnut oil). It did, however, enjoy a stable and nonautocratic government since independence, and France maintained the West African franc (franc CFA) as a convertible currency at a fixed rate. Senegal received large inflows of development assistance (including sizable grants and loans from OPEC nations) and $552 million in loans from official sources, which stabilized its balance-of-payments. Because of the geopolitical importance of the airport in Dakar (it is the point in Africa closest to North and South America and served as an important waypoint for British supplies during the Falklands War), it was likely that OECD aid would continue. In the absence of these political

---

[4] Cohen, *Banks and the Balance of Payments*.

[5] All nations wanted to adjust gradually to the oil shock, but only those with access to credit were able to do so. See Sachs, "Current Account and Macroeconomic Adjustment" and "Oil Shocks and Macroeconomic Adjustment in the United States."

[6] IBRD, *World Debt Tables, 1991–92*, vol. 2. By 1990 Senegal's debt to private creditors had shrunk to $181 million, and it owed $2.8 billion to official sources.

considerations, it is unlikely that French and American banks would have led syndications of large loans to Senegal. And in the absence of such syndications, it is unlikely that banks ranging from the First National Bank of Dallas to the Industrial National Bank of Rhode Island would have proffered to Senegal millions of dollars of their depositors' money.[7]

Aside from consideration of credit risk (economic and political), it is striking how much lending can be predicted on the basis of past history. The major borrowers of the 1970s were also the major borrowers of the 1960s and of the 1860s. Although credit risk evaluation helps to explain which LDCs would receive loans, it does not predict which nations would repay their debt. Indeed, once banks began to converge on the same set of potential sovereign borrowers as their customers, and the funds offered to those countries mounted exponentially, it became less and less likely that an LDC borrower would be able to repay such large sums. The economic rationale behind lending to LDCs does not justify such lending as economically rational. Latin American nations with the promise of export earnings have been borrowing and defaulting in international capital markets since fifty years before the invention of the first oil well.

So markets both did less than is commonly thought and more than one would expect. Markets were an important repository for OPEC funds, but by no means the only one. U.S. government obligations, foreign aid agencies, and international institutions were also important destinations for OPEC capital. Markets did not intermediate between savers and borrowers so much as they determined who the borrowers would be. These determinations seem to have been based on history and political patronage. That is, the agency of market institutions was path-dependent and not based on market-related criteria. The exceptions were oil exporters who chose to run trade deficits for quick industrialization or because the government squandered its new source of funds.

Were Petrodollars Recycled?

If markets did not recycle petrodollars—that is, they did not serve as passive intermediaries—then it might be useful to ask whether petrodollars were, in fact, recycled. In the field of international relations, theo-

---

[7] "Conventions de crédit de réfinancement êntre la République de Sénégal, certaines banques agissant en tant que créanciers, et Citicorp International Bank Limited," mimeo, Dakar: "10/11/82" (11 October or 10 November), pp. 56 and 57.

ries normally start with the assumption of anarchy, or a state of nature, and then explain how it is mitigated. A shared view of anarchy is what allows us to group disparate theorists under the label "realist," yet their central point is not to claim that the world is anarchic but rather to explain why, given the state of nature, the world is ordered. Liberals view anarchy as cooperative and unproblematic. The epistemology of both realism and liberalism is to set out an initial view of nature and then say why it does not really matter. We know that the world is anarchic according to the first meaning of anarchy—lacking a centralized government—and we tend to argue that the world is not anarchic in its everyday usage—chaos and disorder.

Rarely do theorists approach the question of anarchy from the opposite direction: that we live in a world that is more chaotic and anarchic than we think. Although there are many reasonable explanations for petrodollar recycling, I would like to consider the "counterveridical" argument as a partial antidote to the tendency to ignore disorder in theories of international relations.

This book began by posing the problem of recycling as a Prisoners' Dilemma, and this definition of the problem was shared by both policy makers and academics. The empirical evidence presented in Chapter 4 shows that there was a marked lack of cooperation among industrialized nations for both trade and finance. Yet, although responses to the oil shock by industrialized nations were not characterized by cooperation in the first few years following 1973, the world did not sink into another great depression. If there was no cooperation, and mutual defection in a Prisoners' Dilemma is expected in anarchy, should we not describe the outcome as anarchic?

The answer is a definite "maybe." On the one hand, the Prisoners' Dilemma is an overly simplistic model of the challenges of petrodollar recycling. The industrialized world was not a closed system in which defection meant a welfare loss by all. Instead, competitive trade policies resulted in shifting the global trade deficit to the Third World. The "sucker's pay-off" was not to be had by any of the players in the industrialized world, though many of them might have been better off in the long term if all cooperated.

A second way of looking at the Prisoners' Dilemma of trade and finance for recycling is that the United States provided a public good but made its allies pay for it. The United States solved the transfer problem by convincing the largest OPEC surplus holder (Saudi Arabia) to place its capital in government obligations. This, in effect, meant that the United States could print money to buy oil and, further, it could print money to buy European goods and services. To the extent that the United States began negotiating a multilateral agreement on recycling (the Safety Net), it retained its dominance by proposing that funds first come to U.S. markets, then be recycled through the fund to Europe with American conditionalities.

In both of these explanations, the Prisoners' Dilemma is not sufficiently accurate as a model of what nations wanted and did to be helpful to either policy makers or academics. The Prisoners' Dilemma is very useful as a part of language to communicate easily situations in which the Nash equilibrium is sub-Pareto optimal. Beyond using the term as an act of speech, I have little reason in this book to pursue the term to its various logical contortions.

In the solution to the Prisoners' Dilemma where the United States provides a public good, but pays for none of it, one would have to say the petrodollars were recycled. In the previous explanation, however, where all participants defected and the deficits were shifted onto the weak nations of the Third World, it is more difficult to justify the unintended outcomes of power and wealth with any description other than anarchy.

When I was an undergraduate student, Robert C. Tucker tried to teach me that Marxist theory is essentially Hegel stood on his head. I did not understand Hegel when he was standing on his feet, so this did not help me much. Because Alex Wendt's work is a bit easier to understand than Hegel's, I will risk describing my argument about anarchy as "Wendt stood on his head."

Wendt argued that anarchy is a practice constituted by states, and therefore the implications of anarchy are also constructions by state actors.[8] I argue the reverse. Much of what we observe in the international arena is, in fact, anarchic. It is anarchic in the sense of "chaotic" in addition to a lack of central government, which is obvious. Students of international affairs learn that it is ordered because they are taught that "markets work" or that "institutions matter" or that regular patterns of authority and behavior order the self-help system. But these explanations are wrong, and the objective facts do not lend them credence. Because an objective analysis of facts infirms these explanations, I claim that they are falsely imposed intellectual constructions of order. So long as we can believe explanations for how the world works, we can believe that anarchy is order.

Instead of arguing that anarchy is a set of social constructions, as

---

[8] Wendt, "Anarchy Is What States Make of It."

Wendt does, I argue that explanations of order are (sometimes) falsely imposed on events, which incapacitates our ability to recognize order. As opposed to Wendt and to many other critical theorists, I do not agree that all explanations are intellectual impositions and that all should be equally privileged. Some explanations are more convincing than others; some are more objective than others. Some are right and some are wrong. The explanation that market forces worked to recycle petrodollars is in large part wrong. If economists can say that markets are working to produce outcomes, even when there is little logic or meaning to the process by which markets work, then we have no way of differentiating between anarchy and order.

It is possible that we falsely impose order on chaos by imposing intellectual constructs on sets of events that do not deserve to be imbued with meaning. In fact, there is no such thing and never has been such a thing as a "state of nature" in which people's lives are solitary, poor, nasty, brutish, and short. Primates live in social groupings. Monkeys in the forest live in societies. Even ants live in biologically determined societies. But the society of nation-states is more primitive than any human in prehistoric bands ever had to endure. Perhaps we should recognize anarchy for what it is, rather than engage in post hoc legitimations of solitariness and brutality.

Markets as Political Speech

Markets "worked" insofar as they did not collapse, and transactions continued to clear. The idea that the international system of finance might have collapsed is not so farfetched as it might seem from the vantage of hindsight. Federal Reserve officials were afraid that there might be wild swings in the money supply or even market collapse in the mid-1970s. When Bankhaus Herstatt and Franklin National collapsed in 1974, they defaulted on interbank loans that were supposed to be relatively risk-free.[9] The interbank market threatened to stop functioning just at the point when an influx of OPEC funds made it most necessary. The inability of markets to handle OPEC funds was predicted by bankers, Federal Reserve officials, and the CIA.

When bankers face a decline in confidence in their institution, the last thing they are likely to do is to give the public a pessimistic appraisal of the bank's future. Instead, bankers tell the public that there is nothing to worry about and that their deposits are safe. The motivation behind such statements is clearly to bolster public confidence.

[9] See Spero, "Guiding Global Finance."

Public officials and bankers had the same motivation in 1974. They feared that the financial system might fail, but they restricted such fears to confidential memorandums. In public statements, they proclaimed just the opposite: that markets were working and were capable of recycling petrodollars. In reality, the interbank market in July 1974 was operating at half the level of before the Herstatt and Franklin National collapses. A Federal Reserve official told the U.S. Treasury that the bankers' acceptance market had "dried up," and smaller banks were unable to place acceptances in the interbank market.[10]

To bolster confidence in the international financial system, officials made strenuous efforts to direct OPEC funds into Fed coffers. They also made a series of public statements assuring everyone that markets were working. Thus when public officials claimed that markets were working, the reason was that they feared precisely the opposite. In this instance, at least, the claims that markets worked constituted political speech, and it was motivated by anxiety that markets would not work at all.

Markets as a Power Outcome

Policy makers in the United States agreed that the legitimate response to the challenges of petrodollar recycling was multilateral cooperation. Multilateral cooperation had been a cornerstone of financing balance-of-payments adjustment since the Bretton Woods agreement. Rather than competing for capital, nations were supposed to cooperate both to supply and demand adjustment funding.

When William Simon, as treasury secretary, justified the U.S. response as "letting market forces work," he changed the system of how nations were to finance balance-of-payments. Letting market forces work stood in stark contrast to the authoritative distribution of adjustment capital that was supposed to take place in multilateral institutions. By imposing market forces on a situation where multilateral cooperation was supposed to predominate, Simon got other nations to submit to market forces when they would not otherwise have done so. In this sense, the fact that markets were supposed to work was in itself a power outcome.

A pure market is an anonymous, reciprocal, and symmetrical set of power relations between individuals who respect each other's property rights and who accept the price mechanism as the allocative framework

---

[10] See Chapter 2, note 31.

for distributing the value being supplied and demanded.[11] Far from being a state of anarchy, or a natural condition, the market comes about only through complex social conventions.[12] What differentiates market exchange from other subsets of power and makes it reciprocal and symmetrical is the aspect of social conventions that lead us mistakenly to call markets "voluntary." It is social convention that tells us when markets are legitimate means for the distribution of value.

We are not supposed to bribe politicians, and neither are they supposed to buy votes. The allocation of grades in a university should not be subject to market exchange. Children are not anyone's property, and therefore they should not be bought and sold. There are many types of value that are distributed by many social schemes. Some involve pluralism and democratically endowed authority, some involve merit, and some involve complete randomness (or what we call natural factor endowment). And one further social scheme for the allocation of value is market exchange.

We call market exchange "voluntary" because we understand it to be a legitimate way to allocate value and because of the social conventions that we call property rights. If we enjoy property rights, then we perceive our choice as one of exchanging money or goods for something we would rather have, or keeping the money or goods. Because others respect our right not to exchange property and share our understanding that market exchange is a legitimate way to induce the disgorging of property, we are free to volunteer property for exchange, and property is offered for exchange voluntarily. A mugging is not an example of market exchange because the mugger does not respect property rights and because threats of violence are not a legitimate scheme for allocation of money. By the same token, when market exchange is viewed as a choice between participation in a commercial network and starvation or homelessness, it does not seem so voluntary after all.[13]

Property rights are recognized in international politics, but they are not guaranteed. And since the international polity is characterized as a society with shared social purpose and conventions to a much lesser extent than most domestic polities, the legitimacy of allocative mecha-

[11] This definition is inspired by Baldwin, *Paradoxes of Power*, chap. 2, which suggests that it would be more useful to consider economic exchange as a subset of power than to think of power as a symbol of exchange. Baldwin also suggests the notions of the legitimacy of market forces and the symmetry of economic power relations.

[12] Kratochwil, "The World as a Shop."

[13] Polanyi, *Great Transformation*.

nisms is far more problematic. What seems coercive about a mugging is the lack of agreement over property rights and the legitimate means of distributing value, and it is for these reasons that much of international politics seems to be characterized by coercion. What differentiates market exchange from mugging is shared intersubjective understandings of legitimacy.[14] These legitimate notions are important because they help us to analyze power, not because they enable us to predict what sort of power relations will occur.

It is obvious from the briefest examination of international politics that norms of legitimacy are broken constantly. The normative framework in which international politics takes place is important because it helps us to interpret power, not because it determines outcomes. The normative framework is constantly violated, yet that does not negate the fact that it exists. After all, if we deny that morality exists, then we are unable to argue that the world is less than moral. If legitimate understandings do not exist, then we cannot claim that international politics is illegitimate.

We understand power within a normative framework precisely because power is so often used to violate that framework. The important aspect of power that a normative framework enables us to analyze is the difference between market exchange, intervention in allocative systems, and intervention in markets. To know how power is exercised, we must know what an actor would have done in the absence of power relations. To understand how the exercise of power changes an actor's expectations about the consequences of his choices, we must know what framed his expectations to begin with. Both of these points make necessary the study of an actor's counterfactual future and the social environment that led to that future. Once we understand that people are free to withhold their wealth from the poor and homeless as they choose, then we can understand why a panhandler does not have power until he threatens someone with bodily harm. If social conventions obligated people to give money to the needy, then our analysis of a person walking by a panhandler might be a bit different.

Just as it is a power outcome when a teacher sells grades, so too the imposition of markets on the recycling process was a power outcome. It is only by understanding both power and markets in the intersubjective framework in which they occur that we are able to distinguish markets from politics. In the case of petrodollar recycling, a part of the market process was itself a political outcome.

---

[14] Habermas, *Communication and the Evolution of Society.*

Automaticity

In a classic piece that was meant to illustrate the spontaneous development of complex markets, R. A. Radford wrote of Stalag VIIA during World War II, in which prisoners of many nationalities developed a complex system of money based on cigarettes.[15] The fact that the prisoners of war had all grown up with the social conventions of European and American capitalism is not relevant for economists. To them, social relations create a functional need for markets, and markets both arise spontaneously and work automatically.

Yet the actual meaning of markets, property, and exchange differs from society to society. A communal tribe without property rights might barter gold for steel but might not recognize any property rights on food, feeling that market mechanisms are inappropriate for the distribution of nutrition. While market exchange seems to be a form of human social interaction, the context and meaning of the exchange varies so much from group to group that we should not think of it as a natural state. After all, violent force is an even more common form of human interaction. Violence as a fundamental characteristic of international affairs is so obvious that we do not need to study prisoners of war in order to illustrate how it comes about "naturally." Yet we do not privilege violent force as a goal for the international political economy.

The presumption that markets function automatically produces a tautological tendency to credit anything that happens with market forces. For the case of petrodollar recycling, one might easily argue that banks neither recycled nor served as intermediaries. They acted individually to produce an economic outcome that was collectively irrational. The petrodollars that were deposited in markets were not allocated according to any agreed-upon principles or any consistent set of explainable causes. Petrodollars did not flow to nations that needed them to pay for higher oil bills, and indeed there is no market-based reason for why they should have. Petrodollars were not lent to nations likely to repay what they borrowed, even though the banks tried to make such assessments. Although we can explain some of the lending that took place, a large part of the flow of petrodollars through markets did not have any why or wherefore. Markets did not recycle; they did not allocate value based on consistent and agreed-upon principles.

It is a common mistake of observers of the international political economy to assume that since something happened it deserves to be im-

---

[15] Radford, "Economic Organisation of a P.O.W. Camp."

bued with meaning. There is every indication that the ways that markets allocated valued made no sense, and recycling did not take place. If we allow for the possibility that the question is false to begin with, then it is possible that markets did not work to recycle petrodollars because petrodollars were not recycled by any agent.

Although markets did not work to recycle petrodollars and did not intermediate between oil-surplus and oil-deficit countries, they did "work" in two senses of the word. First, markets did not collapse. They were not immobilized so that institutions would neither accept deposits nor lend money. Second, they allocated value in ways that are subject to explanation and postdiction (i.e., prediction of past events without the advantage of hindsight). Banks lent to countries that appeared at the time to be good credit risks. The evaluation of credit risk was based on expectations of future export earnings, political stability, international patronage, and past history.

In sum, to say that markets worked has several meanings, which may extend to cases other than petrodollar recycling. First, funds were directed toward financial institutions, and thus the location of funds (but neither agency nor explanation) involves markets. Second, markets were supposed to function as intermediaries between savers and borrowers, but this meaning supposes that the distribution of balance-of-payments surpluses and deficits is a given. Instead, markets had unanticipated agency in determining where deficits would fall. Third, the claims that markets worked were political attestations, motivated by the desire to inspire public confidence in markets and fueled by fears that markets would fail. Fourth, market forces were a power outcome. In a system in which balance-of-payments adjustment financing was to be distributed by cooperative agreement in multilateral institutions, imposing the market system was a function of America's dominant position in the world. Finally, saying that markets worked is effectively imposing an intellectual construct on a set of events that may have less meaning than we attribute. The way that scholars of international relations normally approach knowledge is to point out and explain elements of order in an anarchic world. Lest we become too confident, there is also value in taking the opposite tack: to point out the degree to which the world is chaotic and bereft of meaning. Market forces can easily be a catchall explanation for whatever happens, even if it lacks meaning.

INSTITUTIONS

Recycling as a Test of Liberal Institutionalism

International institutions did not seem to have much efficacy in the process of recycling, despite the constituted role of the IMF and attempts to form a financial safety net under the auspices of the IEA. I argued in Chapter 4 that institutions did not make information more transparent and did not reduce transaction costs. And I argued throughout this book that the interests of the various actors were quite divergent and often disconsonant. It may be, then, that petrodollar recycling is not a very good test of liberal institutionalism.

According to Keohane, two key conditions must exist if the institutionalist view is to be pertinent.

> First, the actors must have some mutual interests; that is, they must potentially gain from their cooperation. In the absence of mutual interests, the neoliberal perspective on international cooperation would be as irrelevant as a neoclassical theory of international trade in a world without potential gains from trade. The second condition for the relevance of an institutional approach is that variations in the degree of institutionalization exert substantial effects on state behavior.[16]

Unfortunately, it is not entirely clear whether these conditions exist for petrodollar recycling. We know that the world would be better off if all nations lived in peace and harmony, but that is not the same as asserting that mutual interests exist. If it were the same, then it would be impossible ever to identify conflicts of interest. States had conflicting interests for the issue of petrodollar recycling, even though they might have been better off collectively if they cooperated. In that sense liberal institutionalism does not pertain because there was not a strong mutuality of interests. But given the rarity of strong mutuality of interests in any issue area in the international political economy, it is not clear why liberal institutionalism should ever pertain.

If petrodollar recycling does fit the prior assumptions of liberal institutionalism, then it infirms the theory. Liberal institutionalism is either a faulty theory of international political economy, or it is irrelevant to the dominant problems of cooperation. The question of how states cooperate when they want to do so may be an interesting one, but it is very narrow in scope and utility. The major problems facing both theorists

---

[16] Keohane, *International Institutions*, pp. 2–3.

and practitioners of international relations are either not explained or not addressed by liberal institutionalism.

International institutions and regimes with the responsibility for addressing problems such as petrodollar recycling existed at the time of the oil shocks and had a nascent capacity for recycling, but no institution played a significant part in the recycling process. The International Monetary Fund was the most likely candidate for recycling. By 1973, the IMF lacked the resources and capacity to respond to international economic shocks. It did manage to set up two oil facilities and a supplementary financing facility (the Witteveen facility), all of which were primarily devoted to funding oil-related trade deficits in LDCs. Borrowing from the oil facilities was linked to how much of an increase in the price of oil imports each borrowing nation faced, so the oil facilities were to be petrodollar recyclers in the most simple and direct sense. But one-third of the funds went to Italy and the United Kingdom (which did have access to private capital markets), and Saudi purchases of U.S. government obligations were more than the oil facilities attracted from all sources combined.

The reason that the IMF did not play a larger role in recycling petrodollars is that it lacked resources, and the reason it lacked resources was, first and foremost, competition from the United States government. The United States consistently vetoed large quota increases for the IMF. The IMF could have turned to nations for funding at market rates, but even that was made difficult by U.S. competition.

Faced with a choice between investing in U.S. government obligations at market rates or lending to the IMF, it is clear why the Saudis were not entirely enthusiastic about the oil facilities. IMF members no longer shared the perception that the pursuit of profits by central banks was to be subordinated to contributing to the capacity of an international arrangement for economic stabilization. Central banks, rather than member states, were the agents of lending, and if the IMF was to garner funds for temporary facilities it had to compete with capital markets and with the bilateral deals made by borrowing governments such as the United States. The legitimation of markets as intermediaries (despite the fact that these markets did not always intermediate) meant that market forces now affected how the IMF mobilized resources.

The United States also made it difficult for the IMF to borrow from the Saudis by objecting to granting Saudi Arabia a temporary director's seat. In 1978 U.S. treasury secretary Michael Blumenthal made a complex deal with the IMF and Saudi Arabia whereby it was allowed to double its quota, and it could appoint a director for the duration of the

Witteveen facility. In return, the Saudis agreed to keep oil priced in dollars rather than switching to a currency basket or to SDRs.

Although the IMF tried to maintain its responsibilities in the face of these new constraints, it was ultimately unable to defend itself as an institution against the aggressive tactics of its largest member. The IMF was a failure at recycling because international norms had changed to legitimatize outcomes produced by international capital markets and because it lacked the resources to finance balance-of-payments adjustment in a period of severe imbalances. Wealthy nations received more than 60 percent of IMF lending from 1974 to 1976. To the extent that the IMF did intermediate between surplus and deficit nations, the direction and scope of financing were determined by the international distribution of capabilities.

Three other institutions and regimes also had the potential to play a prominent role in petrodollar recycling. At the broadest level, the annual economic summits among leaders of the seven largest industrialized democracies (G-7) provided forums for the routinization of ad hoc agreements. Because these summits were characterized by disagreement and conflict, they served little purpose for petrodollar recycling except for the expression of how leaders viewed legitimate responses to the oil shocks. The summits deferred the problem to the OECD, which in turn led to the creation of the IEA and attempts at policy coordination with OPEC aid donors in the Development Assistance Committee (DAC). Arab aid to LDCs would have been the most direct form of recycling, and the DAC was in the best position to coordinate the allocation of this aid. For developed nations, members of the IEA negotiated a proposal for a Financial Support Fund (the OECD Safety Net). It was to borrow from the repositories of OPEC surplus capital (either capital markets or OECD governments) and relend the funds to oil-deficit nations. According to William Simon, American participation in the Safety Net would "convey unmistakably our commitment to cooperation in preservation of a liberal and open world economic order."[17] The Safety Net was not ratified by Congress.

Cooperation for the G-7 encompassed three major areas. First, no nation was to compete to bring its trade account into balance unilaterally. Second, the largest advanced industrialized democracies were to collude as an oligopsony to suppress the OPEC price of oil. Finally, no na-

---

[17] Testimony of William Simon, U.S. Congress, Senate, Committee on Banking, Housing, and Urban Affairs, *Financial Support Fund*, p. 11.

tion was to compete unilaterally for OPEC capital. In all three areas, co-operation was defined as collusion to fix markets. Cooperating nations promised to prevent unilateral pursuit of economic interests. Participants in the summits agreed that pursuit of economic interests would lead to a socially suboptimal outcome, as in the Prisoners' Dilemma game, rather than the optimal outcome of a hidden hand in international markets.

Each of these three areas was characterized by defection and cheating rather than cooperation. All of the advanced industrialized nations competed to bring their trade accounts into balance immediately after agreeing not to. Cooperation to act as a consumers' cartel was weak and was never actually implemented. Cooperation to avoid competition for OPEC capital resulted in plans for the Financial Support Fund (the Safety Net), which must also be considered a failure.

The Safety Net was a design for recycling to advanced industrialized democracies, which left open the possibility of taking funds out of international and domestic capital markets or borrowing from member governments. It was a mutual assistance pact in the way that the GAB was, but as OECD nations lost voting shares in the IMF it was presumably easier for them to negotiate within the OECD. The direct cause for the failure of the Safety Net to come to fruition was the reluctance of the U.S. government to submit the treaty to Congress for ratification and funding. A more general reason was that the Safety Net institutionalized ad hoc arrangements that already existed, and there was little obvious pretext for bureaucratizing those arrangements in a new and formal international agreement.

Members of the OECD were assigned quotas in the $24 billion Safety Net, and they were to be allowed to borrow their quotas with the agreement of nations with two-thirds of the total quota. With the agreement of nations holding 90 percent of the total, members could borrow double their quota. All borrowing was to be subject to strict conditionalities on free trade and fair exchange rates. The Safety Net was a carrot for nations that would otherwise be tempted to solve their problems by competitive depreciation and restrictive trade. Because the United States was to have 27.8 percent of the vote, it could have unilaterally vetoed the applications of members for loans of double their quotas. To veto any borrowing whatsoever, the United States had only to gain the agreement of any one of the next five largest members (Germany, Japan, France, the United Kingdom, or Italy). Funds were to be taken from wherever OPEC placed its surplus, or if markets were in disarray funds could be provided by the member nations according to their assigned quotas.

In essence, the Safety Net was to serve as an intermediary between markets (which clearly were assumed not to intermediate for the purposes of this proposed fund), and deficit nations in the First World. What proposals for the Safety Net really meant, however, was that the United States government would intermediate between markets and its OECD partners, as was already the case. Since the bulk of OPEC funds ended up in dollar-denominated assets, the U.S. government was already a de facto intermediary. So long as OPEC surplus states sold oil for dollars and then held dollars in financial assets (rather than spending them on goods and services), the United States could in effect print dollars to buy oil. Other nations, which could not print dollars, had to sell their goods and services to the United States in exchange for dollars, or they had to turn to international capital markets to borrow dollars.

Given the abject failure of international institutions to recycle petrodollars, what are the implications for the theory of liberal institutionalism? Is it infirmed by this evidence, does the theory predict the failure of institutions in an instance such as petrodollar recycling, or is this empirical evidence simply irrelevant to the theory? The answer is a combination. The theory is infirmed, but the evidence is not a very good test.

In none of the institutions, regimes, or proposals for institutions does one find that transaction costs or the costs of information were very important. The only substantive result from the IEA was information and the publication of data. This made life more pleasant for academics who studied the oil shocks, but it did little to change the international environment for government actors. The information that the IEA made available to national governments did not enable those governments to keep their agreements. It is unlikely that lack of information or monitoring would have affected the competitive trade practices that the G-7 engaged in.

Neither was the diminished role of the IMF in financing balance-of-payments adjustment dependent in any way on information or transaction costs. If anything, the IMF was hurt by the permanence of its institutional structure insofar as OECD nations, which had previously created the GAB under IMF auspices, preferred by the 1970s to negotiate deals among themselves in a temporary and less formal setting. Keohane has written that "it would count against my theory if most agreements made among governments were constructed not within the framework of international regimes, but on an ad hoc basis."[18] For the

---

[18] Keohane, *After Hegemony*, p. 219.

specific issue of petrodollar recycling, at least, it would seem that governments preferred an ad hoc basis.

The failure of the Safety Net demonstrates that institutions may raise transaction costs rather than lowering them. The United States preferred ad hoc arrangements to an institutional setting, and the difficulty in constructing the Safety Net stemmed from the high cost of creating an institution. In "Institutionalist Theory and the Realist Challenge after the Cold War," Keohane makes the eminently sensible suggestion that institutions are "sticky." Because it is difficult both to construct and to liquidate institutions, they often change their roles to suit changing demands. The March of Dimes became an eleemosynary organization for ending birth defects after polio, its original reason for being, was conquered.[19]

This persistence of regimes and institutions implies that there is a high entry cost. If states benefit from the existence of institutions, and institutions provide that benefit by furnishing information and lowering transaction costs, it is not clear why there should be a high cost for creating institutions. It is not difficult to observe institutional persistence, but it is less obvious that institutions really do lower transaction costs, which is confirmed by studying the institutions observed in this book. Persistence is confirmed by the attempts of the IMF to adapt to new challenges and to a changing role. Yet this persistence cannot be successful if a leading member of the institution blocks change.[20] If persistence reflects previous hierarchies of capabilities, and the leading member uses that lag in recognition of hegemonic decline to affect adversely the efficacy of the institution, then the persistence of institutions serves only to increase their dysfunctionality in the international political economy.

Ironically, the analogy of market failure that liberal institutionalism holds as the problematic to be solved by cooperative regimes was nearly true in the most literal sense. Cooperation was required precisely because of the fear that markets would fail to do their job, yet in the political relations between nation-states there was no failure of the authoritative "market." Cooperation was defined by statespeople as collusion to defeat market outcomes, both for the price and supply of oil and for the

---

[19] Keohane, "Institutional Theory."

[20] In addition, as Peter Katzenstein was generous enough to point out to me, the secrecy of the United States in the arrangements it made to recycle petrodollars raised transaction costs by making information more difficult to obtain. Just as there is no evidence that international institutions lowered transaction costs to promote cooperation, there is ample evidence that the American pursuit of secrecy was antithetical to both institutional multilateralism and international cooperation.

allocation of surplus OPEC capital. The perverse outcomes produced by the pursuit of individual interest were in no way solved by an automaticity of cooperation.

In fact, for the small community of advanced industrialized democracies, the failure to cooperate did not result in a collectively worse outcome. Trade wars among the G-7 pushed the deficit onto smaller OECD economies and LDCs. Competition for capital resulted in success by the United States and did not destabilize the international economy except in the normative sense of delegitimating American hegemony. The advantage to the industrialized nations in institutionalized collusion to fix markets was not so manifest as to create an overwhelming demand for international regimes.

The Future of Multilateralism

While markets and international institutions played minor roles in the direct recycling of petrodollars, bilateral deals between G-7 and OPEC governments were common. Recycling was necessary only insofar as nations agreed to share part of their structural trade deficit with OPEC, and the preponderance of bilateral government deals were aimed at balancing the trade account. Further deals enabled G-7 nations, and the United States in particular, to garner much more OPEC capital than was necessitated by the oil-related deficit on current accounts. These deals violated nearly every agreement that G-7 governments made with each other and represented widespread defection. Despite this failure to cooperate, economic stability was maintained for two reasons. The first was that the penalties of defection were suffered by other OECD nations and by LDCs, not by the largest economies. Those weaker nations bore the structural trade deficit with OPEC. A second reason was that the largest defector was the United States, and since competition for OPEC capital was a zero-sum game, the gain of the United States was a loss for all other nations. To call this hegemonic leadership would be to endow U.S. unilateralism with unintended beneficence, but it preserved economic stability nonetheless.

Competition among advanced industrialized nations to improve exports to OPEC began almost as soon as they had promised each other not to compete. By 1975 Germany had reached a trade surplus with half of the members of OPEC, and by 1977 it was in surplus with all of OPEC. Similarly, the United Kingdom, which had been in deficit to OPEC before the oil shock, reached a surplus by 1977. Given Great Britain's persistent trade deficits during the 1970s, this surplus represented profound effort. France was in surplus with four of the twelve members of OPEC by 1978, partly because it devoted more labor to attracting capital than to selling goods. Japan never reached a trade deficit with OPEC, but it began large and persistent trade surpluses with the rest of the world in 1976.

In the United States, promotion of trade with OPEC took place under the auspices of joint economic commissions. These commissions solved part of the problem by exporting huge quantities of arms to Iran and Saudi Arabia (and later to Oman and Iraq). The joint economic commission for Saudi Arabia also served to steer large infrastructure projects to American firms.

The joint economic commission was also the vehicle by which the United States attracted Saudi capital into American markets in general and U.S. government obligations in particular. The United States was not the only government to recruit OPEC capital, but it was indubitably the most successful. France secretly offered tax advantages to the Kuwaiti government investment funds in the 1970s and secured balance-of-payments loans from SAMA. This was not a violation of any agreement because the French had refused to join its OECD partners in promising not to compete for OPEC capital. The French defected, as they are wont to do, but they never had agreed not to. The U.S. government, by contrast, had "continually stated in the OECD that we would take no special discriminatory action that would attract OPEC funds to the U.S."[21] It was through the joint economic commission that William Simon negotiated the add-on arrangement, whereby SAMA bought U.S. government obligations outside of the normal Federal Reserve auction.

In return, the U.S. government promised to maintain secrecy about Saudi investments. Although congressmen objected to the secrecy of the investments, there was little popular resentment. One might imagine that the public debt of a democratic government should not be sold in secret and that the public would want to know which foreign governments hold the debt. But Federal Reserve auctions of government obligations are not a matter that concerns the average American, and the concerns of congressmen failed to ignite popular disquietude. As Martin Mayer has pointed out,

> The Monday evening news on the networks tells people how much the Dow Jones Industrial Averages went up or down that day, but not . . . the rates at that day's weekly auction of U.S. Treasury bills—though the money spent

---

[21] Schotta to Bosworth.

to buy the Treasury bills at this one weekly auction exceeds the total trading in the Dow in the entire $31\frac{1}{2}$ hours that the market is open each week.[22]

OPEC members are no longer major purchases of U.S. government debt, and the United States has continued to obfuscate publicly available data on German and Japanese official holdings of U.S. paper. The American public is largely unaware of what is happening. The people who would seem to care most are foreign statespeople, and they do not vote in American elections.[23]

Aside from one memorandum by a Treasury Department official to Henry Kissinger outlining the add-on agreement, there is no paper trail explaining what the United States government promised Saudi Arabia in return for its purchases of Treasury paper. As risk-averse investors, the Saudis may have been predisposed to buy Treasury bills in any case, and the add-on agreement was only a marginal incentive. Yet other risk-averse investors such as Kuwait did not place nearly as much of their surplus capital in U.S. government accounts. It is likely, therefore, that the Saudis were convinced by an informal political deal. One former ambassador confirmed that the United States promised Saudi Arabia a security umbrella in return for placement of Saudi capital in U.S. coffers. My research is unable to present any further corroboration of such a promise, but it makes sense and it explains why the Bush administration sent five hundred thousand young Americans to make the world safe for feudal desert monarchy. (I find any other explanation based on American interests to be less than convincing.)

Whatever the motivation of SAMA in directing its funds to the U.S. government, this book does not make the claim that American actions were exploitative of Saudi Arabia. The argument is that such actions were a unilateral incentive to attract OPEC capital, in violation of U.S. agreements with its OECD partners. This unilateralism continued across administrations. It was not simply the devious policy of Nixon and Ford officials, but rather the predictable policy of statespeople who acted in the interest of a declining hegemon.

The Carter administration foreign policy establishment was heavily influenced by the Trilateral Commission and espoused a commitment to multilateralism and policy coordination. Yet during that administration the add-on agreement continued, and government officials jealously continued to guard the secrecy of Saudi investment data. As evidence of this continuity of unilateralism, Treasury Secretary Michael

---

[22] Mayer, *Stealing the Market*, p. 2.

[23] Possible exceptions are some precincts in Chicago and Miami.

Blumenthal advised the director of Central Intelligence that the CIA needed to be more secretive about Saudi investments. The data that the CIA had released, prompting Blumenthal's concern, had already been published by the Dow Jones news service. Further evidence came as Blumenthal sought to convince the Saudis to keep pricing oil in dollars instead of switching to a currency basket. In return, the United States ceded temporary power to the Saudis in the IMF. These policies clearly represented the sort of bilateral government deals that the United States had promised to other advanced industrialized democracies that it would not pursue.

Carter administration officials truly believed in the efficacy of multilateralist norms. They told the public that they were pursuing multilaterism. They made agreements in multilateral forums, and cooperated in summits such as the Bonn Accord. But the outcomes they achieved were unilateral. Their actual policies tended toward unilateralism, and the outcomes they produced tended toward anarchy.

How can we claim that academic multilateralists such as Joseph Nye and Richard Cooper, both of whom were officials in the Carter administration, believed themselves to be pursuing cooperative outcomes while they were responsible for unilateral policies? For one thing, it is my argument that systemic changes in structure led to changes in agency, and I believe that officials such as Nye and Cooper truly attempted multilateralism, but to little avail. The Bonn Accord, for instance, was an honest attempt at multilateral cooperation, but as Kenneth Oye convincingly argues, the policies each state ended up pursuing probably would have come about in the absence of agreement, and changes in the external environment after the Bonn Accord forced states to follow unilateralist policies.[24] It is, indeed, admirable that academics who are appointed to office subordinate their personal views to the national interest and then remain open to differences of opinion upon their return to the academy.

The norm of multilateralism was recognized by the principal actors recycling petrodollars, but the practice of recycling was bilateral. This finding clearly contradicts the writing of scholars such as John Ruggie, who argue that multilateralism in the international political economy is on the rise.[25] I believe that the contradiction arises from the emphasis this book places on distinguishing norms from practice. What policy makers say and what they do are quite different. Ruggie's previous work

[24] Oye, *Economic Discrimination and Political Exchange.*
[25] Ruggie, ed., *Multilateralism Matters.*

made the important observation, following Polanyi, that the norms on how objects of value are distributed are consciously rewritten during transformative periods in history. The late 1970s was such a period. As the exercise of U.S. hegemony became more exploitative, the normative institution of how value was allocated shifted to markets and bilateral deals.

HEGEMONY

Interpreting Hegemony

To examine the nature of power outcomes that effected petrodollar recycling, this book employed a method of determining the intersubjective framework in which power was exercised. The behavioral description of power makes three implicit arguments about the subjective bases of power. The statement that A gets B to do something she would not otherwise do implies that A intends B to do something different, that A causes a change in B's subjective understanding of the situation, and that B would otherwise do something framed by the social constructions of what people or states normally do. If markets are normally the manner by which value is allocated, then participation in markets is not viewed as a form of coercion. Yet if some other legitimate scheme exists for the allocation of value, then the ability of one actor to impose market solutions on other actors is a form of power.

Only by observing what shared understandings exist for the legitimate allocation of value may we interpret how power outcomes change with variation in the international distribution of capabilities. To evaluate American unilateralist policies for petrodollar recycling in terms of hegemonic stability theory, it is necessary to observe how those policies diverged from agreed-upon conventions on how states were to respond to the challenge of recycling.

American policy makers viewed the challenge of recycling as a Prisoners' Dilemma requiring multilateral cooperation. If markets were allowed to function freely, states would bid up the price of oil and would compete for capital. Cooperation, therefore, was defined as collusion to defeat market forces. No state was to make bilateral deals with oil producers because that would raise the price of oil, aggravate the problem of who was to bear trade deficits, and make financing scarce for balance-of-payments adjustment financing.

The legitimate process for responding to the oil shocks was, therefore, mutually exclusive with the free functioning of markets, and it was antithetical to bilateral government deals with OPEC. American policy makers made explicit agreements to avoid giving unilateral incentives to oil producers in order to balance trade or to attract the capital surplus. The forums for recycling were to be international institutions and policy coordination by means of international summitry. If states were reluctant to endow the IMF with a permanent continuation of its Bretton Woods role to intermediate between nations with capital surpluses and deficits, then at the very least they were to create a temporary Safety Net for recycling among OECD nations.

Intervention in international capital markets was to be in the guise of multilateral agreement. American policy makers did not expect that markets would have the capacity to accept the OPEC capital surplus in an orderly fashion, and they envisioned that the Safety Net would take funds out of markets and direct the funds toward nations that needed capital for oil-related trade deficits. An international institution was to perform this intervention in markets. Each OECD nation (except for France) agreed repeatedly that it would not offer oil producers unilateral incentives.

The American response was to offer unilateral incentives and to justify its sabotaging of international institutions as "letting free markets work." Never before in the postwar era had free markets been empowered as a means of distributing balance-of-payments adjustment financing. Market forces were not previously considered a means of allocating value. Instead, these tasks were left to the authoritative decisions of the IMF—a hegemonic regime created and maintained by U.S. leadership. It was U.S. leadership in the 1970s that led to the demise of the IMF as a principal focus for balance-of-payments finance.

The American response to the challenges of petrodollar recycling was, therefore, exploitative of its hegemonic position. Letting the market work, to the extent that it meant OPEC capital would flow to American markets and to the U.S. government, was a power outcome. It varied from the legitimate means of recycling both in the making of explicit agreements and the intersubjective understandings of U.S. policy makers that were revealed by their justificatory attestations. The unilateral nature of the American response was also in contravention of agreements and the intersubjective understandings of legitimacy.

The clearest evidence that the United States acted in a unilateral and self-interested manner, incommensurate with the milieu goals of multilateral cooperation, was the process by which it competed with international institutions. The IMF would have had much greater responsibility in both recycling and world finance in general had the United States not prevented it from taking on the role. Another viable plan was the OECD Safety Net, which American administrations were unwilling to push through Congress. Faced with a choice between legitimate leadership of multilateral regimes and unilateral policies that were solely in the interest of the United States, policy makers chose the latter.

My argument is that such a unilateral response can be predicted for a hegemonic power in decline. As the costs of abiding by the constraints of legitimate leadership in the present outweigh the future benefits of cheaper hegemony, the dominant state with a short future will chose the short-term option of unconstrained self-interest. The dominant position of the United States in the world economy allowed it to garner the bulk of petrodollars and to recycle them on its own terms. This exploitative temptation would be present for any state and would have been present for the United States before it began a process of decline. It was the hegemonic position of the United States that allowed it to offer unilateral incentives and to compete with international institutions. The process of decline freed the United States from the bounds of legitimate leadership and led U.S. policy makers to put to work the hidden hand of American hegemony.

REALISM AND CONSTRUCTIVISM

Imagine what would happen if a teacher walked into a college classroom and began to sell good grades to students. Students would be indignant, and rightfully so. They would claim that grades are supposed to be distributed on the basis of merit and teachers are not to discriminate among rich and poor students. Those with wealth should not be given an unfair advantage by being able to purchase grades. Furthermore, the meaning of a good grade would be denigrated if all teachers sold grades. Our rules, norms, and social conventions do not permit the distribution of grades by means of the price mechanism.

Now imagine that a student walked into a used automobile dealership and attempted to use the same set of arguments. Cars are not distributed on the basis of merit. Used car salespeople are supposed to discriminate between wealthy and poor, insofar as they are to sell to the highest bidder. And a group of used car dealers could possibly collude and argue that if cars were to be sold at lower prices it would hurt the value of used cars, but we would call that price-fixing, and it would be against the law.

What makes a market mechanism appropriate for the distribution of cars and inappropriate for the assignment of grades is the set of values and social conventions that form our expectations. If an actor could substitute authoritative exchange, when we would expect and sanction market mechanisms, we would call that action power. A less well understood but equally valid form of power is when an actor can substitute market mechanisms for authoritative exchanges. When participants in the international political economy expect value to be allocated by the agreement of governments, but when one of them (such as the U.S. government) is able instead to "let market forces work," that actor exercises considerable power.

In the realm of international finance the United States, in three different phases, has exercised considerable power. In the first phase, the immediate postwar era (1944–58), the United States shaped an international system that reified the social conventions by which value was to be allocated. The result was a set of institutions, markets, and patterns of behavior that embodied principles of who got what, when, and where. In the second phase (1958–71), the United States participated in the system and maintained it. In a system where value was allocated, for the most part according to authoritative agreement, the United States served as a legitimate authority.

Beginning in the early 1970s, the United States exercised a third form of power in the realm of international finance: U.S. foreign policy has been characterized by active intervention in the system, and that intervention often has been to the unilateral benefit of the United States. Ironically, this intervention has often entailed permitting markets to produce the outcomes desired by the U.S. government. These shifts in U.S. policy toward market mechanisms are important because international capital flows—which are the basic stuff of international finance—have become central to the stability, smooth functioning, and growth of the international political economy.

It was during the period of petrodollar recycling that the United States government changed the normal practice of how balance-of-payments financing was to be distributed. Before that time, financing took place in an international institution (the IMF) by political agreement. The relative position of the United States in the global economy declined during the 1970s, and its power in the IMF also declined. Yet it was still a dominant force in international markets, and markets produced outcomes favorable to the United States. The new "script" of norms on how financing would be distributed legitimated and empowered markets. Lacking the power to reconstruct political institutions during a period of economic stress, the United States opted for "market forces."

An implication of exploitative hegemony and changing norms is that the United States should have slowed its relative decline, and indeed that is what happened in the 1980s. The shadow of the future for American hegemony once again lengthened, and outcomes represented a new equilibrium between the changed norms and the legitimacy of American leadership. Although the United States is not in a position to implement a new international order after the Cold War, it is in a position to balance once again its particularistic interests with international milieu goals.

This interpretative analysis is impossible with the tools of traditional realist theory. To understand power, we must understand the underlying framework of social conventions and norms that determine counterfactual futures and thus determine when a relationship is one of power. Furthermore, the legitimacy of a power relationship depends entirely on social conventions and norms, particularly when the power involves market exchange. In Dahl's description of power, giving your money to a bookseller is just as much a subset of power as giving your wallet to a mugger. In both cases someone has convinced you to give up your money, which you would not otherwise do. The difference lies in the reciprocal nature of the market exchange (you have made the bookseller relinquish a book, which he would not have otherwise done), the mutual granting of property rights, and the legitimacy of markets for the distribution of books.

Because the manner in which power is exercised in each case depends on the specific expectations and social setting, it is important to specify the context in which power is exercised. Many often speak of the great capabilities of the United States and then are puzzled when the United States does not achieve its objectives.[26] The reason for their puzzlement is that power is often specific to a particular domain. Yet if we are to say anything about power, except as a description of specific situations, we need to develop generalizations about power. A useful compromise is to think about subsets of power relationships, in which scope and domain are specified.[27] For the study of a hegemon's foreign policy and international finance, specific subsets of power relations are best differentiated by the nature of how power is exercised and by the goals for which it is wielded. Among the many subsets of power relations that

[26] Caporaso and Haggard, "Power in International Political Economy."
[27] Baldwin, "Power Analysis and World Politics."

comprise hegemony, three are especially salient for the realm of international finance.

A first subset of hegemonic power comes from what Steven Lukes calls setting preferences, and it is a form of state power that is episodic and rare.[28] After major wars, the international system is reordered so that the hierarchy of prestige by which nations relate to one another reflects the new distribution of capabilities. If one power emerges dominant, it sets the "rules of the game" for the international political economy.[29] After World War II, the United States shaped the principles by which markets were governed with the strange mix of nationalism and internationalism that befitted a strongly isolationist power venturing out on the world stage. In general, this subset of power is the shaping of preferences, rules, and social conventions—that is, the influencing of social purpose.[30] The expectations that determine when markets are functioning "naturally," or when value is allocated according to political authority, are both the result of this first type of hegemonic power.

A second type of hegemonic power entails "letting the system work." Social, economic, and political exchange are carried out in congruence with the conventions, expectations, and rules set forth by the hegemon. Allowing the system to work, however, can be quite different from allowing markets to work (which is called "laissez-faire economics"). For example, if the conventions of the Bretton Woods system call for a political institution (such as the International Monetary Fund) to allocate balance-of-payments adjustment financing, and if instead the United States forces nations to compete for funds in private capital markets, then allowing the market to work directly contradicts letting the system work.

Such interventions in the system are a third subset of hegemonic power, which violates conventions on how power is to achieve outcomes. The third type is differentiable from the second mainly in terms of what social purpose forms the expectations that are the background to power. What constitutes intervention depends on what we expected to happen in the absence of what we called intervention.[31]

Which subset of power the hegemon relies on has much to do with the time frame for its expectations of the future. When there is an absence of social purpose, then it is most likely that a hegemonic power

---

[28] Lukes, *Power*. See also James and Lake, "Second Face of Hegemony."

[29] Gilpin, *War and Change*, chap. 2.

[30] Ikenberry and Kupchan, "Socialization and Hegemonic Power."

[31] The divergence between social purpose and policy is revealed by studying the justifying discourse of policy makers. See Kratochwil, *Rules, Norms, and Decisions*.

will codify international conventions in agreements and institutions. So long as the relative decline that normally follows the first blush of hegemony is not too severe, the "golden period" of hegemony is one of legitimate authority. The leading power is bounded by the precepts of social purpose that it instituted at the start of its rule. It lets the system work because legitimate rule makes future authority less costly. When relative decline does take its toll and the future of hegemonic rule becomes less certain, the hegemonic power may begin to intervene more actively in the system, perhaps by leaving outcomes to international markets (if that serves its purpose). This produces outcomes favorable to the hegemon because of its relative size, despite its decline.

Since the inception of its international leadership role at the end of World War II, the relative position of the United States has undergone very drastic change, and its policy toward financial markets has passed through the four phases of hegemony. The security threats on which the normative framework of the postwar order was based have all but disappeared. It is little wonder, then, that the nature of American hegemony has changed and that the relationship between U.S. foreign policy and international finance presents grave challenges for the future.

The unilateral response of American policy makers to the challenge of petrodollar recycling was motivated by the effects of U.S. relative decline. In the 1970s Treasury officials worried for the first time about how to finance the U.S. budget deficit with foreign savings. If OPEC nations had not run a surplus, the United States would have turned elsewhere. During the 1980s the price of oil fell, and Saudi Arabia began to draw down its account with the New York Federal Reserve Bank. The Gulf War took care of the remainder of Kuwaiti and Saudi savings. The effects of "the market working" came to be known as the LDC debt crisis.

During the 1980s, the United States funded one-third of its new borrowing with capital flows from Japan and Germany. Federal Reserve officials offered Japan the add-on arrangement so that it could buy government obligations outside of the normal auctions. This time there was no need to justify either the add-on arrangement or secrecy. Bilateral deals and extraordinary incentives to attract foreign capital had become the norm for American statespeople.

While there were calls here and there for the United States to stop disrupting the global balance-of-payments by borrowing so much from abroad, neither the G-7 nor any other developed nation seemed to object to the U.S. recruitment of foreign savings into government coffers. Japanese investors were only too happy to buy American securities during their drive to internationalize their financial system. Unfortunately, as wonderful as Japanese management is for its manufacturing sector, the same management techniques give it the worst financial sector in the world. Japanese financial institutions invested in U.S. government securities and then saw most of their investments wiped out by the Louvre and Plaza agreements, which devalued the dollar to the yen.

In the 1990s the costs of German reunification and European monetary integration meant that the United States lost an important customer for its debt. Japan, in the wake of the sandaka shock, sold off $100 billion in U.S. bills, notes, bonds, and securities. Now that the federal budget is balanced, the United States relies less on foreign savings for indebted prosperity.

In the 1970s and 1980s the United States delegitimated its leadership of the international political economy. Its actions weakened international institutions. Today it has regained an equilibrium and is more willing to pursue cooperative policies. But it is not likely that U.S. hegemony will last forever, and the question remains what will happen in the international political economy after hegemony. At this writing, the United States has stopped competing with the IMF and seems more willing to support it as an international mechanism for balance-of-payments adjustment financing. But as willing as the executive branch is to support the IMF, the legislative branch is unwilling to fund it.

In this book, I argue that cooperation after hegemony seems unlikely in the extreme. Petrodollar recycling was unusual in that it was a severe shock to international economic stability. Yet insofar as the oil shocks were a symptom of U.S. hegemonic decline, similar shocks can be expected in the future. International institutions do not have the capacity to handle such threats to stability, and U.S. unilateralism will prevent the strengthening of multilateral cooperative regimes. Although the relative decline of U.S. hegemony has led to an increase in observable power outcomes, the result ultimately will be worldwide economic instability. When it is in a period of relative decline, it is in the short-term interest of the United States to pursue unilateral exploitation of its dominant position. This interest is increasingly at variance with the international goals of confidence, stability, and cooperation.

Works Cited

Achnacarry, Peter. "The Petroleum Crisis, Saudi Arabia and U.S. Foreign Policy." *Energy Information Service* 3 (14 April 1981).

Adams, Donald B., and Heywood Fleisig. "Reduction of Short-Term Capital Inflows from OPEC to the United States." Internal Federal Reserve Study, Division of International Finance, 5 December 1974.

Aliber, Robert Z. *The International Money Game.* 3d ed. New York: Basic Books, 1979; 4th ed. London: Macmillan, 1983; 5th ed. New York: Basic Books, 1987.

——, ed. *The Reconstruction of International Monetary Arrangements.* New York: St. Martin's Press, 1987.

al-Otaiba, Mana Saeed. *OPEC and the Petroleum Industry.* New York: Wiley, 1975.

Art, Robert J., and Robert Jervis. "The Anarchic Environment." In *International Politics: Anarchy, Force, Political Economy, and Decision Making.* 2d ed. Boston: Little, Brown, 1985.

Baldwin, David A. *Paradoxes of Power.* New York: Basil Blackwell, 1989.

——. "Power Analysis and World Politics." *World Politics* 31 (January 1979): 161–94.

Bank for International Settlements. "The Maturity Distribution of International Bank Lending." Press release. Basel: Bank for International Settlements, semiannual.

Bergsten to Blumenthal. Department of the Treasury. Memorandum for Secretary Blumenthal from Assistant Secretary Bergsten, "Briefing for your Meeting with Ambassador to Saudi Arabia, John C. West," 10 March 1978, p. 3.

Blair, John M. *The Control of Oil.* New York: Pantheon, 1976.

Blumenthal to Turner. Department of the Treasury. Letter from W. Michael Blumenthal to Admiral Stansfield Turner, 15 November 1978, on Treasury Department stationery.

Blumenthal, W. Michael. "The World Economy and Technological Change." *Foreign Affairs* 66(1987–88): 529–50.

Bodayla, Stephen D. "Bankers versus Diplomats: The Debate over Mexican Insolvency." *Journal of Interamerican Studies and World Affairs* 24 (November 1982): 461–82.

Branson, William H. "OPEC Lending, LDC Growth, and U.S. Trade." *NBER Working Paper* 791, 1981.

Branson, William H., Hannu Halthunen, and Paul Masson. "Exchange Rates in the Short Run: The Dollar-Deutschemark Rate." *European Economic Review* 10, 3(1977): 303–24.

Brown, Weir M. *World Afloat: National Policies Ruling the Waves.* Princeton: Princeton Essays in International Finance 116 (1976).

Bull, Hedley. *The Anarchical Society: A Study of Order in World Politics.* New York: Columbia University Press, 1977.

Calleo, David P. *Beyond American Hegemony: The Future of the Western Alliance.* New York: Basic Books, 1987.

Capie, Forrest. *Monetary Economics in the 1980s.* Basingstoke, U.K.: Macmillan, 1989.

Caporaso, James A., and Stephan Haggard. "Power in International Political Economy." In *Power and International Relations,* ed. Michael Ward and Richard Stoll. Boulder: Lynne Rienner, 1989.

Caporaso, James A., and David P. Levine. *Theories of Political Economy.* Cambridge: Cambridge University Press, 1992.

Carbaugh, J., and Liang-Shing Fan. *The International Monetary System: History, Institutions, Analyses.* Lawrence: University Press of Kansas, 1976.

Carr, E. H. *The Twenty Years' Crisis, 1919–1939: An Introduction to the Study of International Relations.* London: Macmillan, 1939.

Central Intelligence Agency. Memo from the Office of International Banking and Portfolio Investment, drafted by David Curry, reviewed by F. L. Widman, 21 November 1978, and marked "classified by CIA:DB 312/01645-78, exempt from general declassification schedule of executive order 11652 exemption category 5 b(2."

——. "Problems with Growing Arab Wealth," ER-LR 74-19, July 1974.

——. "Saudi Arabian Foreign Investment." Mimeo, June 1978. The mimeo is marked "Secret, Not Releasable to Foreign Nationals," and was reviewed for declassification in May 1985. It has no other markings to indicate who wrote it for whom.

Chesterton, G. K. "Spiritualism." In *All Things Considered.* New York: Sheed and Ward, 1956.

Cline, William. *International Debt and the Stability of the World Economy.* Policy Analyses in International Economics 4. Washington, D.C.: Institute for International Economics, 1983.

Cohen, Benjamin J. *Banks and the Balance of Payments: Private Lending in the International Adjustment Process.* Montclair, N.J.: Allanheld, Osmun, 1981.

——. *In Whose Interest: International Banking and American Foreign Policy.* New Haven: Yale University Press, 1986.

——. *Organizing the World's Money.* New York: Basic Books, 1977.

Cohen, Edward E. *Athenian Economy and Society: A Banking Perspective.* Princeton: Princeton University Press, 1992.

Collins to Solomon. Treasury Department Internal Memorandum, "CIA Release of Information on Foreign Dollar Holdings," to Mr. Solomon, from J. Foster Collins, Special Assistant to the Secretary (National Security), 19 September 1978.

"Conventions de crédit de réfinancement êntre la République de Sénégal, certaines banques agissant en tant que créanciers, et Citicorp International Bank Limited," mimeo, Dakar: "10/11/82" (10 October or 10 November).

Cooper, Richard N. *The Economics of Interdependence: Economic Policy in the Atlantic Community.* New York: McGraw Hill, 1969.

Corden, W. M. *Inflation, Exchange Rates and the World Economy.* 3d ed. Chicago: University of Chicago Press, 1986.

Dahl, Robert A. "The Concept of Power." *Behavioral Science* 2 (1957): 201–15.

Davis, Steven L. *The Management Function in International Banking.* New York: Wiley, 1979.

Debs, Richard A. "An Address before the Tenth Annual Banking Law Institute in

New York City on May 8, 1975." In *New York Federal Reserve Board Monthly Review*, June 1975, p. 127.

Delamaide, Darrell. *Debt Shock*. London: Weidenfeld & Nicolson, 1984.

De Menil, George. "De Rambouillet à Versailles: Un bilan des sommets économiques." *Politique Etrangère* 2 (June 1982): 403–17.

De Menil, George, and Anthony M. Solomon. *Economic Summitry*. New York: Council on Foreign Relations, 1983.

Dennis, Geoffrey E. J. *International Financial Flows: A Statistical Handbook*. Lexington, Mass.: Lexington Books, 1984.

Department of Commerce. "Request for individual country data from Treasury International Capital reporting on oil-exporting countries" [to and from are blank], 28 November 1978, "Draft" on Bureau of Economic Analysis stationery.

Department of State. "United States and Saudi Arabia to Expand Cooperation." Press release 133, 5 April 1974.

Department of the Treasury. "The Dollar and the Pricing of Oil," a section from a briefing book prepared for Blumenthal's meeting with Saudi finance minister Abalkhail in October 1978.

——. "The Dollar and the Pricing Unit for Oil." Mimeo, 26 October 1978.

——. "Movements in the Relative Purchasing Power of OPEC Dollar Denominated Assets." Mimeo, 23 October 1978.

——. "Saudi Exchange Rate Policy," a single page from a 1978 classified Treasury memo (with no identifying marks except for "Confidential, declassified, authority: Russell Munk, 9/10/79").

——. "Technical Cooperation Agreement between the Government of the Royal Kingdom of Saudi Arabia and the Government of the United States of America," signed at Riyadh 13 February 1975, U.S. Department of the Treasury, TIAS 8072.

Dorfman, Dan. "Kuwait Oil Profits Buy $7 Billion of U.S. Securities." *Washington Post*, 31 May 1981.

Dornbusch, Rudiger. "A Portfolio Balance Model of the Open Economy." *Journal of Monetary Economics* 1 (1975): 3–20.

Doucy, Arthur, and Francis Monheim. "La Révolution dans le domaine des hydrocarbures." In *Les Révolutions algériennes*. Paris: Fayard, 1971.

Eckstein, Harry. *Division and Cohesion in Democracy*. Princeton: Princeton University Press, 1966.

Fraser, Robert D., and Christopher Long. *The World Financial System*. 2d ed. Harlow, U.K.: Longman Current Affairs, 1992.

Frieden, Jeffry A. *Banking on the World: The Politics of American International Finance*. New York: Harper & Row, 1987.

——. *Debt, Development, and Democracy: Modern Political Economy and Latin America, 1965–1985*. Princeton: Princeton University Press, 1991.

Giddens, Anthony. *Central Problems in Social Theory*. Berkeley: University of California Press, 1979.

Gilpin, Robert G. "The Richness of the Tradition of Political Realism." In *Neo-Realism and Its Critics*, ed. Robert O. Keohane. New York: Columbia University Press, 1986.

——. *War and Change in World Politics*. Cambridge: Cambridge University Press, 1981.

Gold, Joseph. *Voting Majorities in the Fund: Effects of Second Amendment of the Articles*. Washington, D.C.: International Monetary Fund, 1977.

Gordon, Richard L. "A Reinterpretation of the Pure Theory of Exhaustion." *Journal of Political Economy* 75 (June 1967): 274–286.

Gowa, Joanne. *Closing the Gold Window: Domestic Politics and the End of Bretton Woods*. Ithaca: Cornell University Press, 1983.

Grieco, Joseph. "Anarchy and the Limits of Cooperation: A Realist Critique of the Newest Liberal Institutionalism." *International Organization* 42, 3 (Summer 1988):485–508.

Habermas, Jürgen. *Communication and the Evolution of Society*, trans. Thomas McCarthy. Cambridge: Polity Press, 1991.

Hall, John A. *Liberalism: Politics, Ideology and the Market*. London: Paladin, 1987.

Hallwood, Paul, and Stuart Sinclair, *Oil, Debt, and Development: OPEC in the Third World*. London: George Allen and Unwin, 1981.

Heal, Geoffrey. "The Relationship between Price and Extraction Cost for a Resource with a Backstop Technology." *Bell Journal of Economics* 7, 2 (Autumn 1976): 371–78.

Helleiner, Eric. "National Currencies and National Identities." *American Behavioral Scientist* 41, 10 (August 1998): 1409–1436.

Hopf, Ted. "The Promise of Constructivism in International Relations Theory." *International Security* 23, 1 (Summer 1998): 171–200.

Hotelling, Harold. "The Economics of Exhaustible Resources." *Journal of Political Economy* 39, 2 (April 1931): 137–175.

Huntington, Samuel. "The U.S.—Decline or Renewal?" *Foreign Affairs* 67, 2 (Winter 1988–89):76–97.

Husayn, ʿAadil. *Al-iqtiṣād al-miṣrī min al-istiqlāl iā al-tabaʿīya, 1974–1979*. 3 vols. Cairo: Dār al-mustaqbal al-ʿarabī, 1982.

IBRD. *World Debt Tables* vol. 1. Washington, D.C.: World Bank, 1989.

———. *World Debt Tables, 1991–92: External Debt of Developing Countries*, vol. 2. Washington, D.C.: World Bank, 1991.

Ikenberry, G. John, and Charles A. Kupchan. "Socialization and Hegemonic Power." *International Organization* 44, 3 (Summer 1990):283–315.

James, Scott C., and David A. Lake. "The Second Face of Hegemony: Britain's Repeal of the Corn Laws and the American Walker Tariff of 1846." *International Organization* 43, 1 (Winter 1989): 1–30.

Johns, Richard Anthony. *Tax Havens and Offshore Finance: A Study of Transnational Economic Development*. New York: St. Martin's Press, 1983.

Johnson, Harry G. "Higher Oil Prices and the International Monetary System." In *The Economics of the Oil Crisis*, ed. T. M. Rybcyznski. London: Macmillan, 1976.

Johnston, Alastair Iain. *Cultural Realism: Strategic Culture and Grand Strategy in Chinese History*. Princeton: Princeton University Press, 1995.

Johnston, R. B. *The Economics of the Euro-Market: History, Theory and Policy*. New York: St. Martin's Press, 1982.

Kambata, Dara. *The Practice of Multinational Banking*. Westport, Conn.: Quorum Books, 1986.

Kapstein, Ethan. *The Insecure Alliance: Energy Crises and Western Politics since 1944*. New York: Oxford University Press, 1989.

Keohane, Robert O. *After Hegemony: Cooperation and Discord in the World Political Economy*. Princeton: Princeton University Press, 1984.

———. *International Institutions and State Power: Essays in International Relations Theory*. Boulder: Westview, 1989.

———. "Intstitutional Theory and the Realist Challenge after the Cold War." In *Neorealism and Neoliberalism: The Contemporary Debate*, ed. David Baldwin. New York: Columbia University Press, 1993.

Keyser to Willett. Appendix ("Memorandum of Conversation") to Internal Treasury Department Memorandum, "Contingency Planning: Consultations with Bankers," from C. Dirck Keyser to Thomas D. Willett, 5 August 1974.

Kindleberger, Charles P. "Dominance and Leadership in the International Economy." *International Studies Quarterly* 25, 2 (June 1981): 242–54.

——. "Hierarchy versus Inertial Cooperation." *International Organization* 40, 4 (Autumn 1986): 841–847.

——. *The World in Depression, 1929–1939.* Berkeley: University of California Press, 1973.

Kissinger, Henry. *Years of Upheaval.* Boston: Little Brown, 1982.

Koslowski, Rey, and Friedrich V. Kratochwil. "Understanding Change in International Politics: The Soviet Empire's Demise and the International System." *International Organization* 48, 2 (Spring 1994): 215–248.

Krasner, Stephen D. "State Power and the Structure of International Trade." *World Politics* 28 (1976): 317–47.

Kratochwil, Friedrich V. "The Embarassment of Changes: Neo-Realism as the Science of Realpolitik without Politics." *Review of International Studies* 19, 1 (1993): 63–80.

——. *Rules, Norms, and Decisions: On the Conditions of Practical and Legal Reasoning in International Relations and Domestic Affairs.* Cambridge: Cambridge University Press, 1989.

——. "The World as a Shop." mimeo, University of Pennsylvania, Autumn 1989.

Lewis, John P. "Can We Escape the Path of Mutual Injury?" In *U.S. Foreign Policy and the Third World—Agenda 1983*, ed. John P. Lewis and Valeriana Kallab. New York: Praeger for the Overseas Development Council, 1983.

Lissakers, Karin. *Banks, Borrowers, and the Establishment: A Revisionist Account of the International Debt Crisis.* New York: Basic Books, 1991.

Logue, Dennis E. "Petro Dollars and Chaos in U.S. Financial Markets." Mimeo. OASIA/Research, Department of the Treasury, 17 June 1974.

Lomax, David F. "The Oil-Finance Cycle Revisited." *National Westminster Bank Quarterly Review*, November 1982: 2–29.

Loriaux, Michael. "The Realists and Saint Augustine: Skepticism, Psychology, and Moral Action an International Relations Thought." *International Studies Quarterly* 36, 4 (December 1992):401–422.

Lukes, Steven. *Power: A Radical View.* London: Macmillan, 1977.

Makin, John H. *The Global Debt Crisis: America's Growing Involvement.* New York: Basic Books, 1984.

Mattione, Richard P. *OPEC's Investments and the International Financial System.* Washington, D.C.: The Brookings Institution, 1985.

Mayer, Martin. *Stealing the Market.* New York: Basic Books, 1992.

McKenzie, George W. *The Economics of the Euro-Currency System.* New York: John Wiley, 1976.

Miller, Judith. "U.S. Securities Draw More OPEC Dollars." *New York Times*, 22 September 1977, A1.

Molière. *Le bourgeois gentilhomme, comedie-ballet, en cinq actes.* Paris: Hachette, 1976 (1670).

Nau, Henry R. *The Myth of America's Decline: Leading the World Economy into the 1990s.* New York: Oxford University Press, 1990.

Nordhaus, William D. "The Allocation of Energy Resources." *Brookings Papers on Economic Activity* 3 (1973): 529–576.

North, Douglass C. *Structure and Change in Economic History.* New York: Norton, 1981.

Nye, Joseph S. *Bound to Lead: The Changing Nature of American Power.* New York: Basic Books, 1990.

Office of International Banking and Portfolio Investment, no title, mimeo, 21 November 1978. This memo was drafted and reviewed by men who are listed on other documents as Treasury officials. However, the memo was classified by the CIA, citing "sensitive intelligence sources and methods involved," and was never declassified. It is therefore unclear what agency in the executive branch this was written for.

Oliver, Robert W. *International Economic Co-operation and the World Bank.* London: Macmillan, 1975.

Oye, Kenneth. *Economic Discrimination and Political Exchange: World Political Economy in the 1930s and 1980s.* Princeton: Princeton University Press, 1992.

Palmer and Munk to Blumenthal. Treasury Department Internal Memorandum to Secretary Blumenthal, "Disclosure of Saudi Arabian Assets in the U.S.," to Secretary Blumenthal, from B. Palmer and R. Munk, 18 August 1978.

Pardee to Coombs. Internal New York Fed Memorandum to Mr. Coombs, "Diversification of OPEC receipts into currencies other than the dollar and sterling," from Scott E. Pardee to Mr. Coombs, 28 October 1974. The memo was forwarded to Arthur Burns (Chairman of the Fed Board of Governors) two days later.

Pizer to Bryant. Internal Memorandum of the Federal Reserve System Board of Governors to Mr. Bryant, "Bankers' Views on Oil Money," from Samuel Pizer to Mr. Bryant, 10 January 1974.

Polanyi, Karl. *The Great Transformation.* Boston: Beacon Press, 1957.

Preeg, Ernest H., ed. *Hard Bargaining Ahead: U.S. Trade Policy and Developing Countries.* Washington, D.C.: Overseas Development Council, 1985.

Putnam, Robert D., and Nicholas Bayne. *Hanging Together: Cooperation and Conflict in the Seven-Power Summits.* Cambridge, MA: Harvard University Press.

Quine, Willard V. *The Ways of Paradox and Other Essays.* New York: Random House, 1966.

Radford, R. A. "The Economic Organisation of a P.O.W. Camp." *Economica,* v. 12 (1945).

Robert Morris Associates. *A Guide to Analyzing Foreign Banks.* Philadelphia: Robert Morris Associates, 1988.

Rockefeller, David. "Financial Aspects of the Energy Situation." from the *Congressional Record,* 24 June 1974.

———. "Rough Seas Ahead: The LDCs and the Credit Squeeze." Remarks at the Chase Econometrics Luncheon, New York, 10 January 1980.

Rosecrance, Richard. *America's Economic Resurgence: A Bold New Strategy.* New York: Harper & Row, 1990.

Ruggie, John Gerard. "International Regimes, Transactions, and Change: Embedded Liberalism in the Postwar Economic Order," *International Organization* 36, 2(Spring, 1982): 379–415.

———, ed. *Multilateralism Matters: The Theory and Praxis of an Institutional Form.* New York: Columbia University Press, 1993.

Sachs, Jeffrey D. "The Current Account and Macroeconomic Adjustment in the 1970s." *Brookings Papers on Economic Activity* 1(1981).

———. "The Oil Shocks and Macroeconomic Adjustment in the United States." *European Economic Review* 18 (1982): 243–248.

Samuelson, Paul. *Economics,* 10th ed., international student ed. Tokyo: McGraw-Hill Kogakusha, 1976.

———. *Readings in Economics,* 7th ed. New York: McGraw Hill, 1973.

Schotta to Bosworth. Memorandum for Stephen W. Bosworth, From Charles Schotta, Subject: NSSM 237: The Issue of "Specials," 21 April 1976.

Shultz, George P., and Kenneth W. Dam. *Economic Policy Beyond the Headlines.* New York: Norton, 1977.

Solomon, Robert. "The Allocation of Oil Deficits." Washington, D.C.: Federal Reserve Board of Governors, 1974.

——. *The International Monetary System 1945–1981*. New York: Harper & Row, 1982.

Southard, Frank A., Jr. *The Evolution of the International Monetary Fund.* Princeton Studies in International Finance n. 135, December 1979.

Spero, Joan. *The Failure of the Franklin National Bank: Challenge to the International Banking System.* New York: Columbia University Press, 1980.

——. "Guiding Global Finance." *Foreign Policy* 73:114–34.

——. *The Politics of International Economic Relations*, 3d ed. New York: St. Martin's Press, 1985; 4th ed. New York: St. Martin's Press, 1985.

Spindler, Andrew J. *The Politics of International Credit—Finance and Foreign Policy in Germany and Japan.* Washington: The Brookings Institution, 1984.

Spiro, David E. *Policy Coordination in the International Political Economy: The Politics of Recycling Petrodollars.* Doctoral dissertation, Department of Politics, Princeton University, 1989.

——. "The State of Cooperation in Theories of State Cooperation: The Evolution of a Category Mistake." *Journal of International Affairs* 42, 1 (Fall 1988): 205–225.

Strange, Susan. "What about International Relations?" In *Paths to International Political Economy*, pp. 191–92, London: George Allen and Unwin, 1984.

Suzuki, Yoshio. *The Evolution of the International Monetary System.* Tokyo: Tokyo University Press, 1990.

Swary, Itzhak. *Global Financial Deregulation.* Cambridge: Blackwell, 1992.

Tétreault, Mary Ann. *Revolution in the World Petroleum Market.* Westport, Connecticut: Quorum Books, 1985.

Tew, Brian. *The Evolution of the International Monetary System, 1945–81.* London: Hutchinson, 1982.

Tobin, James. "A General Equilibrium Approach to Monetary Theory." *Journal of Money Credit and Banking* 1 (February 1969): 15–29.

Trilateral Commission. *Task Force Reports: 1–7.* New York: New York University Press, 1977.

Truman, Edwin M. "U.S. Policy on the Problems of International Debt," *Federal Reserve Bulletin* 75, 11 (November 1989).

Tucker, Robert C. *Politics as Leadership.* Columbia, Missouri: University of Missouri Press, 1981.

Tumlir, Jan. "Oil Payments and Oil Debt and the Problem of Adjustment." In *The Economics of the Oil Crisis*, ed. T. M. Rybcyznski. London: Macmillan, 1976.

Turner to Blumenthal. Central Intelligence Agency. Letter from Stansfield Turner to The Honorable W. Michael Blumenthal, 11 December 1978, on Central Intelligence Agency stationary.

U.S. Congress. House. Committee on Banking and Currency. Ad Hoc Committee on the Domestic and International Monetary Effect of Energy and Other Natural Resource Pricing. *Petrodollars: Recycling and Aid Prospects: Hearing before the Ad Hoc Committee on the Domestic and International Monetary Effect of Energy and Other Natural Resource Pricing of the Committee on Banking and Currency.* 93rd Cong., 2nd Sess., 12 December 1974.

——. Subcommittee on International Finance. *International Petrodollar Crisis: Hearings before the Subcommittee on International Finance of the Committee on Banking and Currency.* 93rd Cong., 2nd Sess., 9 July and 12 August 1974. August 1974).

——. Committee on Banking, Finance, and Urban Affairs. Subcommittee on Economic Stabilization. *OPEC's Proposal to Peg the Price of Oil Exports to Special Drawing Rights.* 95th Cong., 1st Sess., September 1977.

———. Committee on Foreign Affairs. Subcommittee on Europe and the Subcommittee on the Near East and Asia. *U.S.-Europe Relations and the 1973 Middle East War: Joint Hearings of the Subcommittee on Europe and the Subcommittee on the Near East and Asia of the Committee on Foreign Affairs.* 93rd Cong., 1st and 2nd Sess., 1 November 1973 and 19 February 1974.

———. Committee on Government Operations. Subcommittee on Commerce, Consumer, and Monetary Affairs. *Federal Response to OPEC Country Investments in the United States (Part 1 — Overview): Hearings before a Subcommittee of the Committee on Government Operations.* 97th Cong., 1st Sess., 22 and 23 September 1981.

———. *The Operations of Federal Agencies in Monitoring, Reporting on, and Analyzing Foreign Investments in the United States (Part 2 — OPEC Investment in the United States): Hearings before a Subcommittee of the Committee on Government Operations.* 96th Cong., 1st Sess., 16, 17, 18, and 26 July 1979.

———. Committee on International Relations. *International Economic Issues: Hearing before the Committee on International Relations.* 94th Cong., 2nd Sess., 19 February 1976.

U.S. Congress. Joint Economic Committee. *U.S. Foreign Energy Policy: Hearings before the Subcommittee on Energy of the Joint Economic Committee.* 94th Cong., 1st Sess., 17 and 19 September 1975.

U.S. Congress. Senate. Committee on Banking, Housing, and Urban Affairs. *Financial Support Fund Act: Hearings before the Committee on Banking Housing and Urban Affairs.* 94th Cong., 2nd Sess., 4 June 1976.

U.S. Congress. Senate. Committee on Finance. Subcommittee on Financial Markets. *Effect of Petrodollars on Financial Markets: Hearing before the Subcommittee on Financial Markets of the Committee on Finance.* 94th Cong., 1st Sess., 30 January 1975.

———. Subcommittee on International Finance and Resources. *Economic Implications of Massive International Capital Flows: Hearing before the Subcommittee on International Finance and Resources of the Committee on Finance.* 93rd Cong., 2nd Sess., 14 August 1974.

———. Committee on Foreign Relations. *Financial Support Fund: Hearings before the Committee on Foreign Relations on S. 1907 To Provide for the Participation of the United States in the Financial Support Fund.* 94th Cong., 1st Sess., 30 and 31 July 1975 and 26 March 1976.

———. Subcommittee on Foreign Economic Policy. *The Witteveen Facility and the OPEC Financial Surpluses: Hearings before the Subcommittee on Foreign Economic Policy of the Committee on Foreign Relations.* 95th Cong., 1st Sess., 21 and 23 September, and 6, 7 and 10 October 1977.

U.S. General Accounting Office. *Are OPEC Financial Holdings a Danger to U.S. Banks or the Economy?* EMD-79-45 Washington, D.C.: Government Printing Office, 11 June 1979.

———. "The United States–Saudi Arabian Joint Commission on Economic Cooperation." Washington, D.C.: U.S. Government Printing Office, 22 March 1979.

Versluysen, Eugène. *The Political Economy of International Finance.* New York: St. Martin's Press, 1981.

Waltz, Kenneth N. *Theory of International Politics.* Reading, Mass.: Addison-Wesley, 1979.

Watson, Maxwell. *International Capital Markets.* Washington, D.C.: International Monetary Fund, 1988.

Washington Energy Conference. "Final Communique." Doc. 17 (rev. 2), 13 February 1974.

Wendt, Alexander. "Anarchy Is What States Make of It: The Social Construction of Power Politics." *International Organization* 46 (Spring 1992): 391–425.

Widman to Solomon. Treasury Department Internal Memorandum to Under Secretary Solomon, "CIA discussions with Press on Foreign Dollar Holdings," to Under Secretary Solomon from F. Lisle Widman, 14 September 1978.

Willett to Bennett. Department of the Treasury. Appendix ("Memorandum of Conversation," 26 July 1974) to Internal Treasury Department Memorandum, "Report on Discussions with New York Bankers Concerning Prospective Problems in International Financial Markets," from Thomas D. Willett to Under Secretary Bennett and Assistant Secretary Cooper, 7 August 1974.

Yarbrough, Beth V., and Robert M. Yarbrough. "Free Trade, Hegemony, and the Theory of Agency." *Kyklos* 38 (1985): 348–64.

——. "International Institutions and the New Economics of Organization." *International Organization* 44 (Spring 1990): 239.

Yergin, Daniel. *The Prize: The Epic Quest for Oil.* New York: Simon and Schuster, 1991.

Index

About the Author

An international business consultant, David E. Spiro has taught political economy at Brandeis, Columbia, and Harvard universities. He lives with his wife and children in Tucson, Arizona. His e-mail address is David@Spi.ro.